Naive
No
More

Naive to Mare

A Scientist Shares
Lessons Learned
from a Lifetime of
Sexual Experiences

CHARLES KYMBAL

NAIVE NO MORE
A SCIENTIST SHARES LESSONS LEARNED
FROM A LIFETIME OF SEXUAL EXPERIENCES

iUniverse books may be ordered through booksellers or by contacting:

iUniverse
1663 Liberty Drive
Bloomington, IN 47403
www.iuniverse.com
1-800-Authors (1-800-288-4677)

ISBN: 978-1-5320-6506-4 (sc)
ISBN: 978-1-5320-6507-1 (e)

Library of Congress Control Number: 2018914796

Print information available on the last page.

iUniverse rev. date: 12/26/2018

$\mathscr{A}$cknowledgement

I want to express my deepest gratitude to my fourth wife Donna for having the patience and understanding of my wanting to write a book of this nature. In addition, Donna has been a professional editor. Hence, she was a great help in reviewing and proofreading my material. I doubt if this endeavor would have been completed without her assistance.

$\mathcal{I}$ntroduction

When I first thought about writing a book, the plan was to make it a collection of personal vignettes. My history includes four marriages and one living-together relationship encompassing a time period of over sixty-five years. Hence, there are many tales to tell that conclude with the story of my marriage to Donna for over twenty-five years. After giving it considerable thought, I decided to concentrate mostly on my sexual experiences. This was done for the following reasons:

Many of the sexual episodes described in this book contain elements of naivety on my part. I was raised in a difficult family environment. Some background history will help explain why I feel this way. I was born in 1930 during the Great Depression. My father worked on the assembly line of a large automobile plant for a modest wage. Nevertheless, by living frugally, he managed to save a considerable amount of money. He lent most of this money to friends and relatives who were in desperate financial straits due to the depression. Unfortunately, most of these loans were never repaid. According to my mother, this loss affected him greatly and permanently changed his personality and outlook on life. As a result, we lived in modest, unfurnished rental houses/apartments that had only two bedrooms and one bathroom. I had no brothers so I slept with my father in old double bed and my only sister slept with my mother. There was virtually no privacy in these living arrangements. This was the case until I went to college.

Due to our limited financial situation, we never owned a car or even had a telephone. We never took vacations as a family. Eating out or going to a movie was a rare treat. When my mother wanted to replace some of the kitchen appliances, my dad told her to get a job and buy them with her own money. So she did. During WWII, she took a job in a factory assembly line where she inspected cork stoppers.

As for sex, my parents never shared a bed. On rare occasions, I could hear them in the bathroom or the pantry. It was a wham-bam encounter that was over in minutes. Love and affection were never displayed either toward each other or to my sister and me. Vociferous arguments were a daily affair for my folks. Not a happy home environment by any standard!

One of my goals in life was to reverse this trend by having a stable, loving marriage and family. This plan, however, took unexpected twists and turns. Looking back on my life, I see that many of the problems I encountered can be attributed to unrealistic assumptions regarding relationships with the opposite sex - in other words, naivete! Hence, the name for this book: *Naïve No More*. Hopefully, the lessons learned from my failed relationships will be of value to others who are experiencing similar problems.

To describe all phases of my life including early childhood, school days, family experiences, my religious background, and my careers would require a book that would be too long. Also, some of my friends have written memoirs for the benefit of their families and friends. Books of this type are usually meaningful to a limited number of people. What I learned from my experiences should be useful to a broader audience, particularly senior citizens. Furthermore, because of the explicit nature of my sexual history, I do not intend to share this information with those who know me. Despite the fact that all of the events described in this book are true, the names of the individuals involved and the locations where they occurred have been changed. This was done to save myself and the other people involved in these stories from embarrassment and for my legal protection.

I realize that you don't have to be a rocket scientist to write a useful book. However, as it turns out, I am a scientist that had a successful career with government and industry.

One final thought. The easiest way to tell the stories of my sexual experiences is to present them in chronological order starting with the earliest childhood events and ending with the present time. So let's get started.

PART ONE

Early Childhood Experiences

$\mathcal{I}$ntroduction

The early childhood sexual experiences that I recall cover ages three through nine. Many of the details of these events are now vague in my mind. However, I feel that what I do remember must be of some significance in my sexual development since they are still in my memory bank.

Mama Disapproves

When I was about three, I was curious about the appendage between my legs. My mother, who came from a conservative Eastern European background, was getting me ready for bed. While sitting naked on a table waiting for her to get my pajamas, I pulled on my little penis to see how far it would stretch. Much to my delight, it looked like a lady with a long gown. When mama returned, I proudly showed her the lady. She was shocked and told me to never do that again. Her words fell on deaf ears. So much for early sex education!

The Little Girl Next Door

The next event that I recall involved the little girl next door. We lived in an ethnic neighborhood where most of the adults were hard working, blue-collar type individuals primarily concerned with surviving the throes of the Great Depression. It was just assumed that married couples would have children, but they were not as preoccupied with what their kids were doing as they are today. Hence, pre-school children didn't have much to do around the house. The little girl next door and I became pals. Her name was Marie. She was cute, petite and usually wore a short, faded dress. Her dark curly hair and brown eyes were typical for someone of Italian heritage. Both of us were about four when we decided to do some body exploring. A car parked in a garage not far from our homes looked like a safe haven. We got in the back seat where she pulled down her underwear. I reached over with my hand and rubbed the softness between her legs. She was intrigued by this sex play and wanted to see my "thing". I had just dropped my pants when my dad suddenly appeared. Apparently, he saw us go into the garage and figured we were up to no good. Using a switch, he smacked my bare butt repeatedly on the way home. Again, so much for early sex education!

The Wet Surprise

An episode occurred when I was about eight. My sister, Eva, had a girlfriend who was sexually precocious. Her name was Stephanie. She was attractive and had an engaging, aggressive personality. She was also well into puberty and very proud of her developing figure - particularly her firm little boobies. One day, when my parents were both out, we decided to play some sex games. The game we played involved putting my hand down Stephanie's panties. Much to my surprise, her crotch was very wet. I pulled out my hand immediately and exclaimed "Oh, it's so gushy!" I thought she had peed in her pants. When I smelled my fingers, I was surprised at the musky fragrance that was not unpleasant. Only much later did I realize she was exceptionally well-lubricated and ready for action. Well, at my age there wasn't any action to be had.

Two Wheels and Sixteen Cents

When I was in the fourth grade, I became friends with a boy who was a few years older. He convinced me that school was largely a waste of time and it would be more interesting to do things with him. In particular, he was planning to build a Soap Box Derby cart. One day, when we decided to skip school, he wanted me to see parts that he acquired for the cart. In his basement, he showed me more than that. He unzipped his pants and proudly showed me an erect penis which he wanted to put in my mouth. I was not interested, so he promptly offered me his cart wheels so I could start building one of my own. I was still not interested so he upped the ante to include all the money he had in his pocket; this amounted to sixteen cents. As noted earlier, my parents were poor so for me sixteen cents was quite enticing. I thought about his proposition but decided to turn him down. It wasn't because I felt that complying with his request was morally wrong - or did I? At any rate, it never happened again because my parents decided to move to a different neighborhood. That was it for Soap Box Derby carts!

$\mathcal{T}$hat's $\mathcal{H}$ow $\mathcal{D}$oggies $\mathcal{D}$o $\mathcal{I}$t

My first sexual experience with my sister Eva occurred when I was about nine. She was almost four years older and had just entered puberty. Her sex hormones were beginning to stir so she was feeling frisky. One day, when both of our parents were away, Eva came over to where I was sitting at the kitchen table. She approached me from the back, hugged me, and dropped her hands into my crotch. I don't recall getting an erection but I do remember that I got quite excited. When she started to leave the kitchen, I scampered after Eva, pulled up her dress, and pulled down her panties. She didn't object and suggested we go to the living room where we could lie on the floor and continue playing. The only thing I could think of was what I had seen doggies doing, namely, to approach her from the rear. Two problems: when I tried to stick my penis into her butt, it became quickly obvious that we needed a lubricant. Luckily, we found a jar of petroleum jelly in the bathroom cabinet. The other problem was getting an erection sufficient to do any good. I sat on the couch and played with my flaccid wiener but was unable to make it firm enough. Eva thought it might be easier to use the front-door opening. She turned over and spread her legs. It didn't look that appealing to me so I decided to give up. That ended sex play with Eva until we were both in our teens.

Lessons Learned from Early Childhood Experiences

The lessons learned from my early childhood sexual experiences may not apply to everyone

Nevertheless, I have concluded from discussing them with others that my situation was not unique and some generalities could apply to many.

1. Sex play among children is common. Curiosity about your own body and those of the same or opposite sex is a normal part of childhood development. This is particularly true among siblings since there is usually more opportunity for such activity.

2. If parents discover their children having sex play, it is harmful to scold them and make them feel guilty. This type of action creates feelings of guilt that can last a lifetime.

3. Early childhood sex education did not exist when I was young. It's not clear to me that courses of this type in grade school really help. Of more concern, in my opinion, is the effect that violence of the type portrayed in movies, TV, etc. has on childhood development.

4. Fortunately, there was no adult involvement in my early childhood experiences. Not only would this be illegal, but immoral. Unfortunately, such activity is not uncommon

in our society. Virtually every day there are reports in the news media about childhood sexual abuses associated with people from all walks of life.

Finally, although some of my early childhood sexual experiences may be bizarre and sometimes humorous, none of them involved forcible coercion by any of the parties. To me, that is a very important element that is reflected throughout this book. With that said, I will now move on to describe my sexual experiences in adolescence.

PART TWO

Adolescence

Introduction

This part of my life covers ages eleven through eighteen. Although adolescence is defined as puberty to adulthood, I am including some stories that rightfully belong in the pre-puberty category. At any rate, the important thing I want to emphasize in this section is the strong influence some of these episodes had on my sexual development during this critical time.

Hayloft Hijinks

Because both of my parents worked during WWII, there was a problem of what to do with my sister and me during the summer. Since my aunt had a farm in a nearby state, they decided it would be a good place for us to go. When I was eleven, several families were also visiting so there was no room for me to sleep in the farm house. As a result, I had to spend the night in the barn hayloft with a couple of teenage boys as well. Sleeping on hay was not so bad except for all the insects one had to deal with. Hence, we slept with our clothes on. In the morning, one of the boys told me to sit next to him. He put my hand on his penis which quickly became hard. He then had me move my hand up and down which I did for several minutes. I'm not sure if he came or not - maybe he finished the job himself. Later that morning, I told his parents about what happened in the barn. Naturally, he vehemently denied doing anything of the sort. I'm not sure who they believed!

Another Farm Story

There was a small river that ran through my aunt's farm where we would occasionally go for a short swim. One day, the kids from a neighborhood farm came over for a quick dip; two boys and their thirteen-year old sister. When she got out of the water, she went behind some bushes to take off her bathing suit and wrap herself with a towel. One of her brothers snatched the towel off her body. There she stood - naked! Her boobies were in the early stages of development. However, the more interesting part was between her legs. She had some pussy hair - something I had not seen before. She was embarrassed but I was thrilled. Sexual feelings were becoming a big factor in my life!

The ABC's of Jerking Off

Nothing more of sexual significance occurred until I was thirteen. I had heard about masturbation from some of the older boys in the neighborhood. They called it jerking off and told how good it felt when you came. Also, they described how, when you came, you ejaculated this whitish fluid they called gizz. That was a true sign that you were becoming a man, so they claimed. I had not experienced anything like that yet, and was eager to give it a try. At home alone, I would play with my penis until it became semi-hard. After many attempts, I finally succeeded in achieving that good feeling. But no gizz! My disappointment prompted me to of jerk off daily. After several months, I was finally able to produce some gizz! Not much, but enough to feel I was now entering manhood!

More About Ejaculation

Jimmy was one of the boys in the neighborhood who was about fourteen and had the reputation of having a very large penis. Also, he claimed when he masturbated his ejaculate could hit the ceiling. Being inquisitive, I asked him to demonstrate his seemingly outlandish feat. So, one day we went to his house. Jimmy sat on the toilet, pulled out his wiener, and proceeded to jerk off. When he came, his gizz squirted up about a foot - far short of the ceiling! Nevertheless, the demonstration was impressive. Not only did Jimmy have a big dick, he ejaculated a lot more fluid than I had ever seen. However, he was quite disappointed with his performance. Perhaps I was an inhibiting factor - one will never know. I do know, however, that Jimmy was very popular with the girls!

$\mathscr{L}$earning to $\mathscr{K}$iss
(AND OTHER THINGS)

Prior to the age of fourteen, I developed serious crushes on several girls who lived in the neighborhood. Unfortunately, none of these early experiences met with much success. One of my problems was my inherent shyness when dealing with members of the opposite sex. In particular, I was concerned about the issue of kissing. How exactly did one kiss properly? How long should a kiss last? Was it OK to use your tongue? I discovered these questions were not unique with me. One of the guys in the neighborhood, Freddie, confessed he had similar concerns and was looking for answers. We decided to experiment with each other. When nobody was home, we would go to my bedroom and start smooching. The kisses were long and usually involved some tongue play. What surprised me, however, was when Freddie put his hand on my crotch and started fondling my genitals. I returned the favor since it seemed like the appropriate thing to do. Neither of us took this sex play any further. It just seemed like a good learning experience that could be used in the future with girls, not guys. This episode of my life didn't make me feel I had any homosexual leanings. I'm not sure about Freddie, however. When we met many years later at a high school reunion, he gave me the distinct impression that he was gay. Apparently, Freddie got a lot more out of our kissing lessons than I realized!

My Sister - The Teaser

My sister Eva had a nice figure with fully-developed breasts when she entered high school at the age of fourteen. She was attractive with light-brown hair and hazel eyes. Her full lips were made even more prominent by bright-red lipstick that she had just started to wear on a regular basis. Eva was always well-groomed and dressed appropriately for girls of her age. Personality wise, she was bright, confidant, and never reluctant to express her opinions. She was also a good student and participated in a plethora of school activities. The curious aspect of our relationship, however, had to do with sex. Eva was an exceptional teaser in this department. Here are several examples:

1. Eva had a considerable talent for art. She attended an art institute located in the city on a part-time basis where she developed a remarkable skill for drawing pictures of people; mostly scantily clad. I enjoyed looking at her drawings/paintings which she brought home in a portfolio. One day, much to my surprise, I found a pencil drawing of a couple going through the various phases of becoming lovers entitled Boy Meets Girl, First Kiss, Getting to First Base (light petting), Second Base (heavy petting) and lastly Third Base (which showed them having intercourse in the missionary position). I told my buddies about this drawing

and they would come over frequently to view Eva's art work. On occasion, when we finished looking at her drawing, Eva joined us in the living room and sat in a chair where she spread her legs far enough so that we could see her underwear. Not only that, she wore a pair of panties that had a quarter-sized hole in them so that we got a glimpse of her pussy hair. For boys just going into puberty, it was a real turn-on! Also related to Eva's art were several pencil drawings of adult females wearing bathing suits. My best friend, John, and I thought the drawings would be much more interesting by erasing the bathing suits and adding nipples and pussy hair. It worked like a charm and served as a great inspiration for numerous jerk-off sessions. Naturally, we had to put these drawings in a safe place, so we hid them under an old ice box in the pantry. Well, wouldn't you know it; my mother found the drawings and blamed Eva for doing such shameful things. Eva denied this and said I was the guilty one. When confronted, I pleaded ignorance; that it had to be Eva's handiwork. My mother never did know who to believe.

2. During her high school years, Eva had a habit of taking a bath and leaving the bathroom door partially open. She did this when my parents were not home and we were alone in the apartment. Anyway, the door was

opened wide enough so I could see her nude in the bath tub. I really believed she couldn't see me peeking since she never said a word. Naive again? On one occasion, after she took her bath, she came out wearing a very thin negligee that probably belonged to my mother. It was thin enough so I could easily see her full breasts and a dark patch of pussy hair. Not a word was spoken. She went into her bedroom, closed the door and that was the end of that. If you're wondering why I didn't pursue this rather obvious invitation to have sex, my only answer is that at some level, I must have felt that incest would be going too far. Besides, at this stage of my life, I was fully ejaculating with what I assume were healthy little sperms that could make babies - and I didn't have a condom! At least not yet; that comes later.

3. Another story involving Eva occurred during her later high school years when she was dating several boys. Frequently, she came home late after a date after everyone else had gone to bed. Still awake, I heard sounds of a manually-operated carpet sweeper moving back and forth. The sweeper was stored in the bathroom. These sounds continued for some time and then abruptly stopped. I concluded Eva was not cleaning the bathroom floor, but rather was using the sweeper handle to masturbate. I wondered why she didn't use an

object that made no sounds. Then I realized she was probably doing this for my benefit - what a teaser!

4. My last story involving Eva is the boldest and most naive. Because our parents worked, we were alone in the flat during after-school hours. Frequently, Eva would use the couch in the living room to ostensibly take a nap. She would lie on her stomach with her skirt hiked up to just below her panties. I found this very sexy and decided to jerk off. Not in private, but right there in the living room - not more than ten feet from where she was lying. I convinced myself that since she was sleeping, she wouldn't know what I was doing. When I came, I used a handkerchief to catch the ejaculate; isn't that being neat! After numerous sessions of this type, I heard my mother say to Eva as she was getting ready to do the laundry, "Your brother must have a bad cold - all of his handkerchiefs are stiff." She replied "Are you kidding? That's not from a cold." How right she was!

Eva went off to college, got married, had kids, and lost her figure. The days of teasing ended. Over the years, however, I realized that this teasing had a strong impact on my sexual development. I learned that the things that most turned me on were in the category of forbidden fruit.

The Impossible Dream

Another notable event occurred during my high school days. My primary sexual activity during this period of my life was masturbating - sometimes as often as three to four times a day. There was no guilt associated with this activity - I just assumed it was normal for a boy my age. However, someone told me about oral sex and how good it felt to get a blow job. Unfortunately, without a partner, there was no one who could do me the favor. So, I decided to try it by myself. At first, it seemed like it might be physically possible if I could just get limber enough. Despite several attempts, I was unsuccessful. So much for solo blow jobs!

Other Girlie Stories

As I mentioned earlier, I developed strong crushes on several different girls when I was in grade school. However, they didn't feel that way toward me which was devastating. I decided not to date in high school to avoid getting hurt again. And, so it was. My best friend in high school was a classmate named John. We did virtually everything together We also spent a lot of time talking about a variety of subjects including science, religion, philosophy, psychology, and of course girls and sex. Unlike myself, John desperately wanted to date girls but he was a short, hairy fellow that girls didn't find very appealing. As a result, we spent a great deal of our time during those high school years talking about girls and sex but not doing anything about it - except for imagination and masturbation. As high school seniors, it was decided to take some action. First, we went to several burlesque shows, and then visited a strip club. The women in the club were beautiful - both in face and body. However, this venture turned out to be very expensive because one was expected to buy drinks for the ladies after they performed. Also, John and I were both underage for consuming alcoholic drinks. We did it anyway if the bartender was willing to serve us without asking for ID. There's the forbidden fruit element again!

One of the most bizarre strip-club incidents, however, occurred when a group of us guys drove downtown to see a movie. On the way back, the car ran out of gas right in front of a strip club. When our driver went to search for a gas station, John and I decided to pay a visit to the place. We were still underage for drinking and didn't have any money to speak of. Nevertheless, we wanted to see the gal who was stripping so we ambled up to the crowded bar and tried to look as inconspicuous as possible. The bartender spotted us and said "What can I do for you boys?" John immediately spoke up and said "We're looking for Big Red." The bartender replied, "I don't know any Big Red." John shot back "Be careful what you say about him - he is well known in the city." This amazing ad lib that John came up with was a mark of genius I thought. After the Big Red incident, we moved away from the bar and went to an area in the club that one could call bleachers. A waitress immediately approached and asked us what we wanted to drink. John spoke up and said "Nothing - my friend has already had too much to drink and he's feeling kind of sick." So, with that bit of interchange, we decided to move out of the bleachers and go to the other side of the bar. While all of this was going on, we were trying our best to watch the stripper do her thing - which included sticking dollar bills down her G-string. Wouldn't you know it! Another bartender approached us to get our order. Only this time, he looked directly at me. I didn't know what to say, so I just shook my head from side to side. John spoke up and said "My friend is deaf and dumb - leave him alone." That worked and enabled us to see the rest of the stripper's performance.

$\mathcal{L}$essons $\mathcal{L}$earned from $\mathcal{A}$dolescent $\mathcal{E}$xperiences

As noted earlier, a number of significant events occurred during my adolescence that affected my sexual development. These events resulted in lessons learned that I feel are relevant to most people of this age group.

1. The most obvious thing that happens during adolescence is the body's production of sex hormones. These hormones, besides producing physical changes to the body, affect one's mental state in a profound way. In my case, the sex drive became very strong and significantly affected my behavior.

2. One of the biggest issues during sex play in the adolescent years is the possibility of pregnancy. To my knowledge, most teenagers did not use birth control measures such as condoms and birth control pills when they engaged in intercourse. The problem, if pregnancy did occur, was how to deal with the situation. Abortions were considered risky and in most cases illegal. Having a baby, on the other hand, was highly impractical due to the limited maturity and poor economic status of the kids involved. Oral sex was not in vogue during these years. I realize that today's situation

is much different. According to reports of incidents that have occurred in recent years, some individuals do not even consider fellatio to be a sex act. Hence, in today's environment, oral sex may prove to be the best approach to satisfying an unmarried couples sexual needs.

3. During my teenage years, sexually transmitted diseases were of limited concern. AIDS was not yet a factor and other STDs (syphilis, gonorrhea, etc.) were not a problem unless you were involved with a prostitute.

4. Taking into account all of these issues led me to conclude that masturbation was the best way to satisfy my sex drive. Years ago, masturbation was considered to be an unhealthy practice. Sex books suggested that one sublimate his or her sex drive by engaging in other activities (such as sports) and/or taking a cold shower. I tried this approach but it didn't work for me. I am sure this was also true for others. Another issue that complicates the subject of masturbation is the religious factor. Some religions consider masturbation to be a sin. Hence, you have the guilt element with which to contend. Since I was not involved with any religion in my teens, this was not a problem for me.

5. Same-sex activities during the teen years should not be viewed as an indicator of gay or bisexual orientation - at least it wasn't in my case. Furthermore, I personally feel

there is nothing wrong or immoral regarding homosexuality. To each his own!

6. Sex among siblings is a touchy matter. The stigma of incest is very strong in our society. It is fortunate that my sister and I never had intercourse during our teen years. Had this happened, feelings of guilt would be lasting.

7. Sex education during the teen years is probably a good idea. However, it is naive to think this type of information will significantly change one's sexual behavior. Saying no to sex until you are married simply doesn't work for most teens; just like it didn't in the campaign against drugs.

PART THREE

College Years

Introduction

My undergraduate college days span a period of approximately five years - ages eighteen to twenty-three. During this time, several events occurred that were life changing. Some were positive and some were negative, but all were important in my journey to adulthood.

*O*ff to *C*ollege

I left home to attend a state university and decided to major in physics. I was still too reluctant to get involved with girls, so my entire freshman year went dateless. The first problem that arose was how to satisfy my sexual appetite - particularly living in a campus house with three roommates. One day, alone in my room, I decided to jerk off. Just then, one of my roommates walked in and said "Oh, I see you're having a little orgy!" Talk about being embarrassed. That was never tried again!

*G*oing to *C* hurch (OFTEN!)

The solution to satisfying my sex needs involved the church that was located next to our campus house. The church was left unlocked with no one in the basement during most of the week. So, I spent many hours there taking care of business. Some people thought of me as being very religious since I was going to church so often. Well, they were partially right. In future years, religion did become a very important part of my life. But that's another story.

The Problem Persists

During my freshman year, most of the guys I knew were dating, particularly on Saturday nights. That made me quite envious so I decided to do something about it. The university had a counseling center that appeared to be a good place to start. My first and only visit was with a female counselor. I told her about my dating concerns and briefly described my unhappy background with the opposite sex. After hearing my tale of woe, she asked - "Do you masturbate?" Shocked and embarrassed by her question, I said yes but didn't go into any details. We talked some more, but she didn't have any concrete suggestions for how to deal with my problem. However, this one session with the counselor convinced me that I needed to change my attitude toward the opposite sex.

A Minor Breakthrough

At the end of my freshman year, a doctor said I had a hernia that should be repaired. During my stay in the hospital, I met a nurse who was petite, attractive and friendly. With some trepidation, I finally got up the nerve to ask her out. Surprisingly, she promptly said yes. We went to an event on campus and then to a local restaurant. Despite her attractiveness, I quickly discovered there was no chemistry for me and concluded there would be no follow-up dates. Not even a good-night kiss! Despite this first-date disappointment, it was a first step in the right direction.

The German Opportunity

During my sophomore year in German class, I met a coed named Pat. Not only was she attractive and well-built, she had a vivacious personality that attracted attention wherever she went. Naturally, she was very popular with the guys including one fellow who was on the football team. It was flattering when she agreed to go out with me. We had several dates that went okay except they were purely platonic. She asked me about my shyness, so I told her about my early unhappy experiences with girls. She was sympathetic and willing to let things proceed at a slow pace. But then the proverbial crap hit the fan! One evening, she told me about a list of the boys she was dating and how they were arranged in order of her preference. And guess what - my name was not at the top! All the feelings associated with my grade school experiences came flooding back. So, that ended the German Opportunity for me.

A Major Breakthrough

Near the end of my sophomore year, a very important event occurred that changed my life significantly. One of my classmates, Jim, told me about a girl, Alice, whom he had known for years. She worked as a secretary for the university and lived with her mother in a house located near the campus. On Saturday nights, she would borrow her mother's car and go to a dance that was held in a small town about twenty-five miles from the university. Jim would occasionally go with her on these trips. One day, he asked me if would like to accompany them. My first reaction was an emphatic no - dancing was not for me! On the other hand, the opportunity was somewhat appealing. So I went.

Alice was tall, thin, and had a receding chin which emphasized her overbite. Also, her breasts were nothing to write home about. Nevertheless, she was attractive when she dressed up and wore makeup. I found her to be non-threatening since she was a small-town girl with no desire to obtain a college education. Therefore, I didn't need to impress her to make any headway. Alice did possess some qualities that were different from other girls I had known. She had a strong-willed personality and was not reluctant to make her desires known. She was also a very good dancer. One Saturday night, she was determined to get me up on the dance floor. As usual, I said no repeatedly. However, when the band took a break, we went to a nearby bar and had several drinks. That did the trick! I got on the dance floor and let Alice show me some basic steps. It was a major breakthrough that resulted in several life-changing events.

Event Number One

After a month or so of going to these dances with Alice and Jim, he dropped out of the picture. I'm not sure if this was his choice or whether she had something to do with it. This gave us a good opportunity to be alone. Since Alice was still using her mother's car, we found we could get the privacy we needed by pulling off into a cornfield. Initially, we just did a lot of kissing and light petting. Her breasts were not large, but it was still thrilling for me to fondle them even if it was through her clothing. When the petting eventually progressed to sliding my hand between her legs, we realized we needed a more comfortable place to proceed further. Her living room was the best choice. With this new location, the heavy petting continued except that now it was more frequent than just Saturday dance nights. So much so that we decided I should move to her mother's house into a rental room that had become available. So, I guess you could say that we were now going steady and were having a good time every night after her mother went to bed. One odd thing occurred during these heavy petting sessions. Alice was reluctant to let me put my hand inside her panties. I tried to convince her the only thing that was keeping my hand from playing with her pussy was a piece of thin cloth - where was the logic in that? At any rate, she finally acquiesced and I could now use my finger to penetrate her body.

Although there was talk about having intercourse, we were concerned about the possibility of pregnancy plus the fear of getting caught by her mother - she wasn't that heavy a sleeper as we found out later! I don't remember how I was being sexually satisfied in these nightly sessions. Oral sex was not even considered - it was not in vogue as it is today. She was probably giving me hand jobs which were okay, but I eagerly wanted to try the real thing.

The Big Event

The sex play with Alice went on for many months. We then decided to throw caution to the wind and go for the big event. The room that I was renting from her mother seemed like a logical place to do it. However, the bed in that room was not very wide plus it squeaked when you sat on it. Not wanting to announce to her mother what we were up to, we decided to put the mattress and pillows on the floor. We stripped off our clothes and laid our naked bodies on the makeshift bed. I had a condom in my wallet since high school days. It had been there so long it left a ring mark on the leather case. Many of the guys had similar wallet rings - it was sort of a badge of honor. I didn't have any experience putting on a condom. The first concern was whether it was still useable. When it appeared to be okay, my attempts to put it on were a bit challenging. You can probably guess what happened - I lost my erection! After waiting all these years to lose my virginity, this was a big disappointment. I felt terrible, but what to do about it? The answer came the following night. We started our usual heavy petting on the living room couch. This quickly resulted in a good erection. No time was spent putting the mattress on the floor or taking off our clothes. With Alice stretched out on the couch, I quickly put my pecker in her and came in a matter of seconds. How was it you might ask? Somewhat disappointing! On the one hand, it was great to feel I was no longer a virgin. On the other hand, Alice seemed blasé about this milestone event. If she had an orgasm, it was not evident. She had also claimed to be a virgin. Again, there was no evidence to support this. But it didn't matter that much to me - I now felt like a man. Mission accomplished!

Event Number Three - Moving Out Time

A few weeks after the big event, Alice and her mother got into a heated argument that resulted in Alice moving out and renting a room near the campus. I decided to move back to the campus house. During this time, Alice was acting quite differently. She was becoming more sullen and unhappy. I began to feel something was basically wrong and perhaps the relationship should be terminated. When I told her about my feelings, she broke down in a veil of tears. She claimed I was just using her as a plaything and saw no future for us. I was quite stunned by what she said and felt sorry for her. Out of pity, I asked her if she would be happier if we were engaged. That seemed to do the trick. During the summer break after my junior year at college, we took a trip to have Alice meet my parents. That didn't go well. They both felt we were too young to get married. Furthermore, they didn't like Alice and said she was too skinny. My dad threatened to stop helping me with my college expenses if I got married before graduating. Despite my parents' negative reaction, I got Alice an engagement ring. That seemed to satisfy her for the time being. However, there was trouble brewing on the horizon!

My Senior Year

My senior year was quite significant regarding the situation with Alice - but not in a positive way. She moved back to her mother's place and continued to work as a secretary at the university. I remained in the house on campus where I had been staying during most of my college days. We got together frequently in the evenings and continued to have sex on a regular basis. Several things happened during this time that caused us considerable concern. First, I was not using condoms. Why, I am not sure. It could have been a cost issue, or that they are bothersome to use and decrease the feeling you get during intercourse. More likely, however, it should be attributed to the folly of youth! Alice was not using any form of birth control so we tried to avoid having sex when she was ovulating. On one occasion, we had sex during her period. What a mess that was! We never tried it again. Unfortunately, Alice's periods were quite irregular. Several times, when she was a few weeks late, we thought she was pregnant. The possibility of an abortion was seriously considered but neither of us felt this would be a good solution; but not for religious reasons. Luckily, she never was pregnant; but it was a very worrisome issue at the time. The second concern was related to the fact that although Alice gave the appearance of enjoying our sex play, she never achieved an orgasm. I just assumed that all women had orgasms at least some of the time. She was not interested in oral sex - either giving or receiving, and she never talked about masturbating - with one exception. One night, Alice's divorced father came over to her mother's house. Alice slept on a cot in her mother's bedroom. When they thought she was asleep, her parents had sex in the same room. Alice pretended to sleep through this whole affair. She found it very sexually stimulating and later used a wooden coat hanger to masturbate. It seems reasonable to assume she achieved some sort of sexual satisfaction even if it wasn't a full orgasm. Another story was also very interesting. Before she met me, Alice and one of her girlfriends went to a drive-in movie and engaged in sex play. They scooted down so other people could not see there were two females; that would not have been fashionable in those days. Her girlfriend proceeded to put a finger in Alice's vagina, then her rectum, and finally, both simultaneously. Again, Alice did not say whether she reached a climax, but it seems obvious that it was a pleasurable experience. I wonder if they watched any of the movie! Hearing about Alice's past sexual escapades turned me on and I encouraged her to tell me more. She was more than willing to oblige. This is mentioned because it became a pattern for me that was relevant in other relationships.

$\mathcal{T}$he $\mathcal{R}$ing $\mathcal{T}$hrower

Another event that occurred during my senior year should have alerted me to additional problems to come in my relationship with Alice. One day, we got into an argument over some issue I have since forgotten. It became so heated that she took off her engagement ring and threw it at me. I picked it up and left in a huff. I pondered for some time whether to end the relationship or apologize and ask her to take the ring back. This was a crucial decision that would have lasting consequences. With considerable trepidation, I went back to see if we could resolve our differences. The subject of love was never discussed - that should have been a big warning sign! Nevertheless, we did eventually agree to get married soon after my graduation.

Lessons Learned from My College Years

There were many lessons that I learned during my college years. However, for the purpose of this book, I have cited only those that had a bearing on my sexual development. Here is a summary of those that I feel are the most significant:

1. Concentrating on studies only during my freshman year was not a good choice for me. The dating hiatus that started in high school made me feel I missed an important part of college life.

2. Seeing a university counselor to discuss my dating reluctance was a factor in changing my attitude toward the opposite sex.

3. In my freshman year, masturbation continued to be my only outlet for sexual relief. I never felt it was sinful or unhealthy and continue to believe that to this day.

4. Dating, which I began to do in my sophomore year, gave my ego a boost. However, competing with other guys for the same girl caused me to feel uncomfortable and brought back memories of early rejections. When I met Alice, who had few if any suitors, this concern was greatly alleviated. Unfortunately, dating her exclusively proved to be a big mistake. I had

very little experience with the dating game and was unprepared for the trials and tribulations of a monogamous relationship.

5. Getting engaged in my junior year was also a big mistake. It was premature and done for the wrong reasons.

6. Having unprotected sex that could have led to an unwanted pregnancy was both foolish and reckless.

7. There were many warning signs that my relationship with Alice was on shaky grounds. That I chose to ignore them is another example of my being naive.

PART FOUR

*Marriage
Number One*

$\mathcal{I}$ntroduction

In 1953, at the age of twenty-three, I graduated from the university with a bachelor's degree in physics and an Air Force ROTC commission. I took a job at the university's nuclear laboratory while Alice, who was a year younger than I, continued to work as a secretary for the school. We rented a small apartment near the campus while waiting for orders to report for active duty with the Air Force. In the meantime, we decided to get married in a local Unitarian church. Part four of this book describes the trials and tribulations associated with this marriage.

Pre-Marriage Problems

Alice and I agreed to have a small wedding with only family and close friends. Everything was proceeding quite smoothly until the time came to send out the wedding invitations. Since Alice's parents were divorced, the invitation listed only her mother's name. When her dad learned about this, he was furious and said he would not attend the wedding nor would he financially support it in any way. Surprisingly, my folks attended the wedding as did three of my high school friends. I was quite nervous about the whole affair and almost passed out during the wedding ceremony. However, things went along okay and we soon departed for a brief honeymoon.

The Not-So-Exciting Honeymoon

When we arrived at our honeymoon destination and checked into the motel, there was no great anticipation about having sex that night. After all, we had been screwing around for more than two years so nothing was new. We did have intercourse in the missionary position and it was not very exciting. Alice still didn't have an orgasm despite my best efforts. So, it wasn't a very memorable honeymoon. A sign of things to come?

The Post-Honeymoon Experiment

After returning home from our uneventful honeymoon, we attempted to spice up our sex life by trying anal sex. This requires good lubrication plus the ability for the receiving partner to relax the sphincter muscle. I'm not sure whether the gel didn't perform as expected or if Alice was unable to relax sufficiently, but I do know it didn't work! I give credit to Alice, however, for at least trying to experiment with new techniques in our sex life. I learned many years later that she was experimenting more than I realized.

The Air Force Beckons

A few months after my graduation, I received orders to report to an Air Force base located in Texas for what they called Indoctrination and Processing. This short episode in my life had two instances where sex was a factor. The first occurred in what was referred to as bachelor officer quarters. Married personnel were not allowed to bring their wives to this base. Hence, I was assigned to a room that accommodated four men. One afternoon, I went to our room to take a nap. A roommate was lying on his bed, pants unzipped, playing with his large, erect penis. Most people would call him very handsome - almost to the point of being pretty. At any rate, he didn't say a word to me and didn't seem to be embarrassed by my presence. Rather, it appeared he was inviting me to engage in some sort of sex play. My response was to say nothing and just pretend I didn't see anything. We never discussed what happened that day so his intentions remained a mystery.

The other instance occurred when we were in our fourth week at the base. Guys can get horny when they have been doing without sex for that period of time. So, it was exciting for a group of us to take a quick trip to a nearby Mexican town to visit the senoritas in a house of ill repute. When we got there, I was impressed with the size and decor of the place. It was larger than any nightclub I had seen in the states and was nicely decorated with attractive drapes and furniture. Although the place looked clean, there was a smell of cigarette smoke which wasn't offensive to me since I was a smoker in those days. When the ladies of the night came out to greet us, I was unimpressed with their looks and figures - on the chubby side to say the least. They wore simple housedresses and little make-up although I did catch a scent of cheap perfume. Their English was limited but adquate to make it clear what they were willing to do for a price. Surprisingly, none of these negative factors fazed my buddies, so off they went with their Mexican playmates to take care of business. These guys were all married, but that didn't seem to matter. I decided to just sit at the bar and drink some beer while I waited for my friends to return. Several women tried to convince me to have sex with them. When I kept refusing, the madam of the house paid me a visit. When she also failed to change my mind, she said in a loud voice, "You know something - I think you're queer!" I just smiled and kept drinking my beer.

I later wondered why I went to this place. The beer certainly wasn't that good. Perhaps I just wanted to see what a Mexican whorehouse looked like. I didn't have sex there for several reasons. First, I didn't find the women attractive. Second, in addition to being concerned about getting a sexually-transmitted disease, this part of Mexico was plagued by a severe water shortage. Hence, showering was not permitted - not a good situation for personal hygiene. Third, having been married for only three months, I didn't think it was right to cheat on Alice.

Off to Mississippi

After finishing my one-month stay in Texas, I received orders to attend an Air Force school located in Mississippi. Having just completed a two-semester course in electronics at the university, the Air Force, in all their wisdom, was now sending me to a six-month course in basic electronics. Most of my days were spent fishing and having a good time - and I still graduated at the top of my class! This was just the first of many screw-ups that occurred during my active duty tour.

When we first arrived in Mississippi, we didn't own an automobile. Alice's dad drove us to the base in a pickup truck and a trailer that held our few possessions. It became immediately apparent there was no way I could get to class on time without a car. So, off we went to a local auto dealer and purchased a used stick-shift vehicle. Problem! I didn't know how to drive. My parents never owned a car so we relied entirely on street cars and buses. The next challenge was for Alice to give me driving instructions. Big mistake! First, we should have never purchased a stick-shift car. Learning how to clutch and shift was not easy for me. Second, the streets near the base were very narrow and congested. Not a good place for driving lessons. Finally, one should never ask your spouse to teach you to drive - you're just asking for trouble. Nevertheless, after several challenging months, I did get my driver's license.

Only one experience occurred during this time that had a sexual connotation. We had heard about a famous gay nightclub located in New Orleans so we took a short trip there to satisfy our curiosity. I was amazed! The guys performing were beautiful with attractive bodies - until they removed their padded bras! Later, we had good sex. I guess one could attribute it to the taste of forbidden fruit we experienced at the nightclub. Back then, many people would consider that sort of activity to be rather risqué. At any rate, this forbidden fruit element was becoming more of a pattern for me as you will see in the following stories.

Westward Ho

When my Air Force electronics course was completed, I was assigned to a base in New Mexico. I was told my schooling would be highly classified and that it dealt with nuclear matters. But first, a top-secret security clearance was required. Since both my parents were born and raised in the Ukraine, which was part of the Soviet Union in the fifties, this undoubtedly created some concern for the agency doing the background investigation. This was particularly true since my dad was sympathetic to the Soviet form of government and was a regular reader of a communist newspaper published in the United States. As a result, six months went by with no clearance notification. During this time, I took a couple of graduate courses in math and physics at the local university. This went very well so I wanted to be assigned in the area to continue my schooling. Unfortunately, the personnel officer didn't agree. After about one year, I finally got my clearance and attended several weeks of schooling at the base on some of the nuclear weapons that the United States had in its arsenal at that time. There were no courses in nuclear physics or any form of graduate school that had been promised earlier. Naive again!

During our stay in New Mexico, Alice got a job as a clerk-typist. We decided she should work for at least five years before trying to have children. At the base, we would frequently go to the Officers' Club where they served excellent food and half-priced drinks. After one of these outings, both of us were feeling no pain having consumed several cocktails. Back home, we decided to try something new in our sex life. Alice agreed to give me oral sex! Much to my delight, I quickly achieved an erection which she took into her mouth. But being inexperienced in this department, she tried to take all of it. She gagged immediately and threw up. What a mess! Anyway, that was the one and only blow job that I got from Alice.

One other sexual incident occurred during our stay in New Mexico. Alice had become friends with a woman with whom she worked. Being single and somewhat lonely, she agreed to let us fix her up with one of my bachelor officer friends. During double dates, everyone seemed to be happy and comfortable with each other. On one occasion, the four of us took a short trip to a near-by Mexican town. After a delicious and inexpensive dinner at a local restaurant, we agreed that it might be fun to take in a show at a nightclub. I hailed a cab and tried to convey our desires. This proved to be quite difficult since none of us spoke Spanish and the driver spoke very little English. He finally understood what was wanted, so off we went to a place that was some distance from town. Upon arriving, we realized this was no ordinary nightclub. It looked very much like the bordello I had visited earlier in Mexico. Inside, there were scores of men lined up waiting for the ladies. They looked at us with curiosity as if to say, "What the hell are you doing here?" After locating the person who seemed to be in charge of things, there was another language problem. He was under the impression that all four of us were looking for sex partners. Finally, we made it clear that we just wanted to see a show. He agreed but wanted a ridiculous sum of money. After much haggling, the price was reduced to twenty-five dollars. Then we got another surprise. There was an extra charge for a dildo to be used in the performance. At this point in time, we were tired of all the confusion and bargaining and agreed to pay the additional fee; on with the show! Two middle-aged women appeared on a small, makeshift stage. Both were unattractive and chubby as well. After both stripped naked, one of them strapped on a large, rubber penis. They then proceeded to have intercourse in a variety of positions and, I have to admit, some were new to me. The climax of the show came when one of them got on her back with her legs spread wide apart. She cackled like a chicken and produced an egg from her vagina! She asked us if we wanted to keep the egg as a souvenir. "No thanks," I said, "We already have enough Mexican souvenirs." With that, we hastily departed with the cab driver that brought us to this so-called nightclub. Alice and I weren't sure how our unmarried traveling companions felt about this whole experience. To the best of my memory, it wasn't discussed at all. However, I do remember it felt very good to be back on U.S. soil.

*O*ther *D*isappointments

When the Air Force training in New Mexico was completed, I received orders to report to a facility located in South Dakota. What a blow! My new position did not require a physics background. Also, it was not possible to continue with graduate work since there were no suitable schools in the area. This new assignment had a minimum commitment of two years which, for the most part, was a waste of my time. Several things happened, however, that were life-changing for me. Since this book is focused primarily on events of a sexual nature, I will concentrate on these.

The unit to which I was assigned was relatively small. Hence, the personnel working there were a rather tight-knit community. Although everyone had top-secret clearances, there were rumors of a considerable amount of hanky-panky going on. This was particularly true of one of the officers who had the reputation of being quite the ladies' man despite being married.

Alice and I decided we still weren't ready to have children and that she should continue to work for several more years. As it turned out, she got a job as a secretary at the facility where I was stationed. Everything seemed to be going along okay except our sex life had become rather boring. To spice things up, we decided to take pictures of Alice in various stages of partial undress. Surprisingly, these were developed at a local photo store without any problems. We were both pleased with the way the pictures turned out and it did seem to add some zest to our sex play. Also, we would occasionally have parties at our base housing unit that had a touchy - feely element. Some of the games we played with other couples included the ladies' man whose name was Doug. I'm not sure about what happened at these parties, but it was clear that Alice was attracted to Doug. This was not too surprising since he was quite handsome and charming in his ways. Several things occurred that led me to think that something funny was going on. First, Alice got an inflatable bra that increased her apparent breast size from a B to a C cup. She wore this bra to work usually with a tight-fitting sweater. Clearly, this was not for my benefit. Second, the photo album that contained the pictures of Alice partially nude suddenly disappeared. She claimed ignorance of where they went. Third, Alice was using a diaphragm for birth control purposes. She used it only before and after we had sex. Otherwise, it was kept in a bedroom dresser. On several occasions, the diaphragm was missing. When asked about it, she became very defensive and claimed it was being used for sanitary reasons. That was news to me! The most suspicious event, however, happened one day when Alice was seen by the gate security guards leaving the base with Doug. They teased me about this funny business since they knew about his reputation. When asked about this incident, she became very defensive again and said she was merely taking him home because his car had broken down. She strongly resented that her fidelity was being questioned. So, I shrugged it off as being possibly true. Naive again!

My assignment in South Dakota satisfied my two-year commitment. Since there was no future for me in the Air Force, I asked to be released from active duty. When the request was denied, I told my commanding officer about my plans to send a letter to a U.S. senator from my home state. This letter would describe in detail how the Air Force had completely misrepresented their initial promises regarding graduate school and their plans to use my physics background. That did the trick. My request for discharge was processed very quickly!

Back to Civilian Life

After completing my active duty tour, I took a position as a civilian working for an Air Force research and development center. At the time, the government was planning to build a nuclear powered airplane. My job, as a physicist, was to help plan in the design and utilization of a new facility that would be used for this program. Alice got a job as a clerk-typist at one of the center's laboratories. Both of us felt she should work for another two or three years before trying to have children. So that's pretty much how things went. The sex was routine and not very exciting.

We became friendly with a couple who lived in the same neighborhood. Friday nights were often spent getting together for dinner and drinks. On one occasion, after having consumed a lot of liquor, Alice stated that she never had an orgasm. This confession was good news to our neighbor's wife who had the same sexual issue. I mention this story because it illustrates two significant factors in relationships. One has to do with alcohol and how it affects most people when they drink too much. They will do and say things they would normally not do when they are sober. This was certainly the case in my relationship with Alice. The second factor has to do with female orgasms. How many women regularly experience orgasms during sex? And how important is it anyway? In my marriage to Alice, I felt she had a problem that needed to be fixed.

$\mathcal{B}$aby $\mathcal{B}$usiness

The time finally came when Alice and I felt it would be nice to have children. After trying for more than a year, she didn't get pregnant. We read a lot of books on the subject that contained instructions on how one could maximize the chances for pregnancy by keeping a close record of ovulation times, body temperatures, etc. The sex became methodical and just plain boring. No fun at all! When it became clear that this wasn't doing the job, I decided to go to a clinic to have my sperm checked. I was unsure what the procedure would be and therefore, a bit apprehensive. The female clerk at the desk handed me a plastic cup and told me where the men's room was located. Somewhat shocked and embarrassed, I took the cup and went into one of the stalls. No help was provided to ease my task. No sexy magazines, videos, or better yet, an offer to give me a hand! I was on my own with a distinct possibility of someone coming into the men's room while I was doing what I had to do. Fortunately, since I was only thirty and horny, it didn't take long to produce a sample. The lab analysis showed that my sperm was in good shape. So that brought up the question of Alice's fertility. After a thorough OB/GYN exam, it was determined that her vagina was not healthy for the little swimmers. Therefore, it was recommended that she use a nutritional douche regularly to correct the situation. Apparently, that did the job and our first daughter was born a year later. But something else had been going on!

More Hanky-Panky

My job required going on a number of out-of-town trips to various nuclear reactor facilities around the country. On one of these occasions, I finished my business early and returned home sooner than expected. Alice was surprised by my early arrival and acted as if she wasn't pleased to see me. I found her behavior puzzling particularly after I decided to have a drink from the only bottle of whiskey we had in the house. It was obvious that quite a bit of it had been consumed during my absence. Alice's response was she needed a drink or two to deal with the pressures at work. When we went to bed later that night and had sex, she was more responsive than usual. Also, the outer lips of her vagina were engorged which, most likely, resulted from sexual stimulation. To my knowledge, Alice never engaged in masturbation since we were married. It sure appeared that some sort of hanky panky had been going on while I was away.

Another event further reinforced my suspicions. About a year later, we attended an office Christmas party at a recreational hall. As usual at parties of this type, there was a lot of drinking and everyone seemed to be feeling no pain. It was a cold night, so when the time came to go home, I went out to the car to get it warmed up. I started the car and waited for Alice. After an unusually long period of time, I went back to the hall that was now quite dark since most people had left. There was Alice and some guy I didn't recognize in a tight embrace. It looked like they were kissing and who knows what else. Enraged, I jumped on this Romeo and knocked him to the floor. After hitting him repeatedly, Alice pleaded with me to stop. She was very upset I would do such a thing when there was no reason to be jealous. The next morning, she said that I had taken advantage of her friend since he was a victim of childhood polio and could not defend himself. She insisted I call him and apologize for my behavior. Reluctantly, I did call him - something that I always regretted. As I later learned, he was in fact screwing Alice for some time before this incident. Another example of being very naive or just plain stupid - or both!

New Location – New Job

In the early sixties, the Air Force decided it no longer wanted to develop a nuclear-powered airplane. They also decided the facility where I was working was no longer needed and should be mothballed. As a result, I quit working for the Air Force. The government was now interested in sending astronauts to Mars. The only way it could be done at that time was with a nuclear-powered rocket. A civilian contractor had been selected to design and build a nuclear reactor that would be the energy source for such a rocket. So, with my interest in things nuclear, I accepted a position with this company at a facility located in Pennsylvania.

When we made the move to our new location, Alice was pregnant with our second child. Conceiving the second was much quicker and easier than the first. Or so I thought. Later, the question of whether I was really her father became a serious issue.

Still More Hanky-Panky

After our second child was born, we purchased a nice house on a hilly, wooded lot in a fairly affluent community. As we got to know our neighbors, someone suggested that it would be fun to have adult-only parties on a regular basis. These parties involved a lot of drinking and dancing until the wee hours of the morning. This produced a fertile environment for flirtatious behavior. What I didn't realize until much later was that for Alice it didn't stop with just flirting.

Apparently, one of the guys, Dick, who regularly attended these events found Alice attractive and wanted to get in her pants. Despite being married, he had no qualms about seeking his sexual delights elsewhere.

During this time, I was active in a Unitarian church which involved a lot of committee/board meetings in the evenings. Alice would use these opportunities to invite Dick over to our house for some heavy-duty petting. I guess they felt it would be too risky to take it to the point of actual intercourse. For this type of sexual activity, they went to a motel during the day when the kids were in a pre-school program. I was not aware of these shenanigans until many years later. Naive again!

The Thousand-Dollar Orgasm

When we lived in Pennsylvania, sex with Alice was quite mundane except when she was having an affair with Dick. As I learned later, their attempts at intercourse were not successful because of his impotence. However, these incidents stimulated her so that sex with me later that day was much more exciting. Despite this surprising development, Alice was still unable to achieve an orgasm. I suggested she visit an OB/GYN to determine if there was a physiological reason for her problem. Rather reluctantly, she agreed. The exam showed nothing abnormal and we were back to square one. I wondered if a significant financial incentive might help. That's when I got the idea of offering her a thousand dollars if she was successful. At first, my offer was not taken seriously. After a while, however, she realized I wasn't kidding and started to think of ways to capture the prize. Apparently, masturbation was not on her list of possibilities. One approach that she tried was to see a woman therapist who supposedly had some success in dealing with matters of this sort. Her advice for Alice was to sit on the toilet and squeeze a wet sponge so the water would trickle down the lips of her vagina! This technique was too weird for her so she never tried it. At any rate, the thousand-dollar incentive didn't work. It was probably naive of me to think it had a chance.

Another Move

During our last two years in Pennsylvania, we moved to a larger house in a different neighborhood. As a result, the late-night couple's parties ended for us. However, Alice's affair with Dick continued. She never told me the details but you can bet they weren't just holding hands. One night, after sex, Alice surprised me. She wanted to know if it would be possible to leave my penis in her after coming. I was under the impression that a man always lost his erection after ejaculating. I later learned that Doug, her South Dakota paramour, was an exception. Apparently, despite having a small penis, he would stay hard after he ostensibly had an orgasm. Also, she said he was able to have multiple orgasms. I was aware some women claim they have this ability, but it was the first time I heard that some men were also capable of this feat. I didn't know if there was any truth to the story. At any rate, this is another example of my being naive about the world of sex and its many ramifications.

Our final years in Pennsylvania included two important activities that were going on simultaneously. First, Alice started taking courses at a local university. Second, I started an evening MBA program at the same school. These were both positive events that gave me hope for the future. Also, our daughters were doing well in school. Then came a real blow! The government decided they were no longer interested in developing a nuclear-powered rocket. Hence, the program I was working on came to a screeching halt. I was not able to find another position at my level with any of the other company facilities in the local area. The only possibility was to transfer to a division in the Baltimore/Washington region. This was a stressful move, but I was still hopeful things would work out for the best. Little did I know what was about to happen!

$\mathcal{T}$he $\mathcal{E}$nd of a $\mathcal{N}$ineteen-$\mathcal{Y}$ear Marriage

The move to the Baltimore/Washington area went quite smoothly. We purchased a nice house in suburban Maryland that was reasonably close to my work. This area was known for being very progressive with a plethora of social and athletic activities. My relationship with Alice, however, had gone downhill. The positive elements mentioned earlier were now gone. Sex was becoming less and less frequent. There were more arguments that were upsetting for both of us. I seriously started to consider ending this unhappy marriage. The greatest deterrent to such a move was my concern about how the girls, now ten and twelve, would be affected. The straw that broke the camel's back came when we took a trip to Florida. Alice was frequently nasty and argumentative during what was supposed to be a fun vacation. When we returned to Maryland, I decided the time had come for me to move out. One morning, I told Alice and the girls about my intention of leaving. That afternoon, I packed a suitcase and checked into a local hotel. This was a very difficult time for me. I was forty-two and had no idea of what the future would be like without Alice and the kids. My next move was to a small apartment in a local farmhouse. On weekends, I would return to the house to take care of any tasks such as mowing the lawn, etc. On one of these occasions, we talked about the possibility of getting back together. My two stipulations were that we get the assistance of a marriage counselor, and that we be entirely honest with each other. Keep in mind that I had serious doubts about Alice's fidelity for many years; suspicions that she vehemently denied every time the subject was brought up. Without hesitation, Alice said she was not interested in my proposal. So, after a month or two of my weekly visits, the time had come to start separation proceedings.

Despite my past problems with Alice, I wanted our separation and subsequent divorce to be as painless as possible. When the time came for her to relocate to a new condo unit, I offered to help her move. After a long and arduous day of getting her settled, she offered me a martini. One drink led to another so both of us were feeling no pain. Alice said she was exhausted and going to bed. I hung around for a while and then decided to do something that makes absolutely no sense but had that tantalizing taste of forbidden fruit. I went into her bedroom and put my hand between her legs. Surprisingly, she did not object and seemed to be enjoying it. She reached out and put her hand on my penis which was now bulging inside my pants. I pulled down her panties and started giving her oral sex - something that never happened during our twenty-one year relationship! Suddenly, the bedroom door opened and in walked our youngest daughter. She quickly retreated when she saw us without saying a word. That ended the sex play and I promptly left concerned about how Alice and the kids would react to this situation.

So what lessons were learned from my relationship with Alice? Not as many as I should have, but these are the ones I remember.

Lessons Learned from My First Marriage and Divorce

My relationship with Alice lasted approximately twenty-one years; including dating and engagement. During this relatively long period of time, I made a number of serious mistakes that taught me the following lessons:

1. It was foolish of me to get involved in a monogamous relationship with very little dating experience on my part.

2. It was even more foolish of me to get engaged when there were many signs that our relationship was not on a good stable foundation.

3. The decision to get married was a bigger mistake. When one commits to a supposedly lifelong relationship, there should be no doubt that you truly love that person and are willing to make the necessary adjustments and compromises that are needed in a successful marriage.

4. Having children can be a useful diversion in a marriage that is on shaky ground. However, one should not assume that it will be the glue to keep a marriage together. One often hears the phrase - we stayed in the marriage for the sake of the children. In my opinion, this is not a good reason to stay in an unhealthy relationship. It's true that divorces can be very

difficult for children to cope with. However, it's even worse if they are exposed to serious marital discord.

5. There is no doubt that infidelities in a marriage can be very destructive to a couple's relationship - particularly in the critical area of trust. In my case, Alice strayed and I did not. Why she chose to have affairs with other men is something I never understood. However, this was not the primary reason for my wanting a divorce. Rather, it was her general negative disposition and nastiness that was more than I could endure. Marriage counseling might have helped but it requires both parties to deal with their problems seriously and honestly. Unfortunately, this was not the case with Alice.

6. Having sex with Alice after our separation was a terrible mistake. It must have been a traumatic shock to my daughter who walked in on us. Plus, I'm sure it gave false hopes to Alice and the kids that we would resolve our problems and everything would soon be back to normal.

7. Fortunately, the divorce process went smoothly and did not invoke any problems in deciding who gets what. I felt good about providing generous child support and sufficient funding for Alice to complete her college education on a full-time basis. I later learned that financial matters can prove to be a major stumbling block in many divorce proceedings.

PART FIVE

Dating Experiences

$\mathscr{I}$ntroduction

Alice and I separated in the spring of 1972. Although we were still legally married, I felt it was okay for me to start dating since I saw no hope for a future reconciliation. I reached this decision because of Alice's rejection of my proposal to obtain the services of a marriage counselor. My dating experiences, which lasted two years, were limited to two women - Pat and Marge. The relationship with Pat was short-lived for reasons that will become clear in the following stories. The situation with Marge, on the other hand, was totally different since it became a monogamous affair soon after we met. Part five of the book deals with this phase of my life which sets the stage for my next marriage.

My First Date - A Near Disaster!

Being single can be a very lonely world - one in which I was very uncomfortable and unhappy. In the early seventies, meeting singles via the internet was not a good option for me. Therefore, I decided to enter the dating game by attending activities of local singles groups. At one of these events, a woman named Pat caught my eye. She was attractive with long dark-brown hair and a decent figure. She was divorced and raising two young boys. Although Pat was shy in her demeanor, she was very friendly to me and seemed willing to strike up a romantic relationship. She asked me about coming to her place some evening. My response was yes anticipating a night of sexual pleasures. After getting to her house, which was a considerable drive from my condo, we had several strong drinks of whiskey. I expected the next step to be a trip to her bedroom. After a bit of light petting, she informed me that we couldn't go any further because her two boys were upstairs in their bedroom. However, she promised me that they would be with their father on my next visit. Somewhat disappointed, I decided to leave. Big mistake! I was still feeling the effects of the drinks and, since it was after midnight, I was very tired and sleepy. On the drive back, there was a state trooper's car stopped on the side of the road. At that point, I nodded off. After regaining consciousness, I found myself headed straight for the trooper. I quickly turned the steering wheel and just managed to avoid hitting him. I was in big trouble - the trooper was coming after me with his lights flashing. When I pulled over and rolled down the window, he angrily said "You know you almost hit me." I agreed with him and attributed my condition to sleepiness. Amazingly, he did not check me for sobriety, but told me to be more careful in the future. I didn't even get a warning ticket! I've often wondered what would have happened to my life if had hit him with my car. It was just a matter of seconds that made the difference.

My Second Visit to Pat

After my harrowing experience, I was reluctant to visit Pat again if it required driving back the same evening. She assured me that with her children gone, I could spend the night. So, off I went to hopefully get some action. We started with drinking and heavy petting on the couch. When she suggested we move to the bedroom, I felt rather anxious since this was a new experience for me. This anxiety prevented me from achieving an erection that I obviously needed for intercourse. There we were, lying naked in bed, and not sure what to do. That's when I decided to give her oral sex instead. When I put my head between her legs, she asked me to stop because it was that time of the month. That struck me as being rather strange since she was willing to have intercourse. I realize that some women enjoy having sex during their periods, but I knew from past experience with Alice that it could get messy. Then, as luck would have it, Pat's car horn started blaring. A hurricane had just hit the area and we were getting torrential rains. Apparently, this short-circuited the car's wiring and caused the horn to activate. Naked as a jaybird (whatever that is), she put on a raincoat and went outside to take care of the problem. The next morning, on the way to my condo, I encountered many flooded areas that made it almost impossible to navigate. All of these problems convinced me this would be my last trip to see Pat.

In the meantime, I met another woman, Marge, who changed the course of my life. Before getting to the story of Marge, however, I would be remiss if I didn't first include some lessons I learned from my dating experiences.

$\mathcal{L}$essons $\mathcal{L}$earned from $\mathcal{D}$ating

I personally found that dating in the singles world was a mixture of good and not so good experiences. Here are the reasons I found this to be the case:

1. Most of the singles I met were looking for a partner with whom they could share the rest of their life. Initially, my intention was to avoid monogamous relationships. Dating several women at the same time seemed to be the best approach for avoiding serious commitments. However, I found this technique had several pitfalls, the worst of which was jealousy. Feelings are easily hurt.

2. With regard to sex, I wasn't sure what to expect from my dating partners. It appeared that if one had a number of dates with the same individual having sex was the norm. I also learned that, for me, having the right sexual chemistry was essential. Some of the women I met were attractive and had pleasant personalities. However, if pheromones weren't present, the relationship remained platonic. After finding an individual where the chemistry felt right, I abandoned the dating game to concentrate on that person. Thus begins the story of Marge.

*M*eet *M*arge

At a singles activity, there was a woman who got my attention. Her name was Marge and, as I learned later, she was divorced and raising two teen-age girls. She lived in a modest row house and worked as an EKG technician at a local hospital. Unlike Alice and Pat, Marge was shorter than I and would be considered petite by most standards. She wore her brown hair in a page-boy style which I found attractive. As for her figure, she was somewhat flat in the rear-end department, but had full breasts that were a delight to behold. When I first saw her, she was sitting on the floor with her legs crossed so that one could get quite a view up her short skirt. On the other hand, she seemed to be quite shy and reserved in demeanor. What I saw was appealing to me, particularly the flesh she was revealing. So, I asked her if she would like to go out. When she agreed, I was pleasantly surprised. On our first date, I was impressed with her appearance which now included blue eye shadow that enhanced her brown eyes; she was even more attractive than when we first met. She was wearing a low-cut blouse that provided a generous view of her breasts and a soft bra that did very little to conceal her large nipples. In addition to her physical attributes, Marge was also intelligent, an avid reader, and had many interests similar to my own. She was a member of the Episcopal faith and went to one of the local churches with her children. When we started dating on a regular basis, I would go with her to church. I found out rather quickly that she was questioning many of the basic beliefs of the Christian faith and Episcopal doctrines in particular. As a result, we started attending Unitarian services. I mention this phase of my life because it opened a new chapter on religion that has profoundly affected me to this day.

Not too long after I met Marge, we started to have sex on a frequent basis. Being in her mid-thirties, she felt that pregnancy was still possible. As a result, we used double protection whenever we had intercourse. She used a diaphragm and I used a condom. On one occasion, after we had sex on her living room floor, I couldn't find the condom! We searched the entire room and each other with no luck. Finally, after being completely baffled, she discovered that the condom had wedged itself behind the diaphragm. Apparently, after I came and lost my erection, the condom slipped off my penis while still inside of her. Then, I must have gotten another erection that pushed the condom where it shouldn't go - so much for birth control! It's funny now, but it wasn't then.

About six months into our relationship, Marge and I had the opportunity to go to Spain. The one-week trip was very reasonable in cost and would be our first overseas experience. We both realized that a trip of this sort would be a great opportunity to get to know each other intimately since we would be sharing a suite in a beautiful hotel overlooking the

Mediterranean. While we were there, we purchased a can of whipped cream. Guess what that was used for! This was oral sex with a twist. It was a little messy but exciting because of being different. On another occasion, we went to the beach and had a nice dip in the sea. When we got out of the water, Marge wanted to get out of her wet bathing suit. Since there were no change rooms on the beach, she proceeded to rap a towel around her and slip off her suit. I'm not sure how she managed to do that but I found it very bold and exciting. This was the gal for me. We both felt that we were on our honeymoon despite the fact that the subject of marriage had never been mentioned. Somehow Alice got wind of our trip and decided that she wanted to work things out between the two of us. She invited me to come over one evening and greeted me at the door wearing a short, sexy nightgown. She asked me if I wanted to watch TV or whether I would prefer seeing her pussy as she slid her panties to one side. I was sorely tempted but somehow managed to say that it was too late for any reconciliation.

Another Big Mistake

After my divorce was finalized, new problems arose that created a very stressful situation for Marge and me. Alice had custody of our two children, but I had visitation rights on alternate weekends. She also completed her schooling to become a RN and was now working full time at a local hospital. This meant the girls were home alone much of the time. As one might expect, this created a ripe environment for them to get into trouble. They were both in their early teens and experimenting with alcohol, drugs, and sex. Alice would call me frequently at Marge's place to say she couldn't take it anymore. She threatened to leave or commit suicide. In either case, the children would be my responsibility. I knew this was something that Marge wouldn't be able to cope with. I was faced with a terrible dilemma. Late one night, after having just left Marge's place, I returned to my condo and heard the phone ringing. It was Alice. She sounded incoherent and spoke very weakly. I assumed she had taken an overdose of something and was in the process of dying. I rushed over to her condo expecting the worst. I rang her bell several times with no response. Through a window, I could see what appeared to be a body lying on the living room floor. So I rang again until she slowly got to her feet and answered the door. To my surprise, she seemed a bit groggy but otherwise okay. To my greater surprise, she started to tell me about her past infidelities of which there were many. Apparently, she felt her confessions would convince me she was serious about resolving our problems. But now comes the amazing part of the story. Instead of becoming upset at what she was telling me, I found myself getting more and more turned on! I wanted to hear all the details she was now willing to share. Forbidden fruit- it tasted so good! She came over to the couch where I was sitting and offered me oral sex. Since I had intercourse with Marge earlier that evening, I wasn't sure how to respond. Without waiting for an answer, she unzipped my pants and put my penis in her mouth. To my amazement, I came rather quickly. When the passion subsided, it became clear how foolish I was. Alice thought there was still hope when, in fact, there was none. I consider this event to be one of the biggest mistakes of my life!

After Alice's failed attempt to end my relationship with Marge, life settled down a bit. Frantic calls from Alice stopped. I would have my girls on alternate weekends and that went okay for the most part. I was still not spending the nights at Marge's place, but rather returned to my condo. This was getting tedious, so we started talking about the possibility of marriage. Both of us knew that second marriages were a serious challenge with a poor record of success. Nevertheless, we had many interests in common and truly loved one another. So, we decided to get engaged before taking the big leap.

More About Marge

After we got engaged, I continued to live in my condo. Many evenings and on weekends, however, I would be at Marge's place. We had sex frequently - usually in the basement den when we felt her girls were asleep in their upstairs bedroom. As we got to know each other better, I saw further signs that Marge liked to play teasing games that had a sexual slant. Quite often, she wore thin bras with see-through blouses that left little to the imagination. She also wore short skirts that made it relatively easy to show her panties when she felt frisky. On one occasion, Marge decided to wear a tight-fitting sweater with no bra. We danced some jitterbug numbers that evening which provided a great opportunity to display her bouncing boobs. These games turned me on and we always ended up having great sex. But then we started to do something that was quite risky.

Risky Games

Marge and I decided we would spice up our sex lives by playing teasing games at local bars. She would remove her engagement ring and go up to the bar by herself pretending to be a single woman looking for some action. It usually didn't take long for one of the guys to take note and approach her to see if she was interested. At this point, I would enter the scene and make it clear that she was with me and off we would go. This type of teasing excited both of us and always led to a night of good sex. On one occasion, we went to a nightclub that was well known as a singles pickup establishment. The place was very crowded so there was a good opportunity to rub against other bodies and cop a feel. Marge was wearing a top with no bra that readily displayed her large breasts and nipples. Naturally, this was noticed by several guys at the bar who were quite vocal in their approval. One of them approached her from the rear and ran his hand between her legs. She was surprised at this action but apparently not dismayed. After consuming several drinks, we both needed to use the restrooms. I noticed that it was taking Marge longer than usual to do her business. When she finally came out and was approaching me in the hallway, she undid her wrap skirt and revealed that she had removed her panties.

I was the only one in the hallway at the time and the pussy display was very short. Nevertheless, she didn't know who might suddenly appear to see the show. I was amazed by her boldness and decided this was the woman for me. Marriage was the next logical step.

PART SIX

*Marriage
Number Two*

$\mathcal{I}$ntroduction

Marge and I were married in 1974. I was forty-four and she was five years younger. Initially, this was a marriage that we both felt would last forever. However, as the following stories reveal, this would not be the case.

Tying The Knot

Although some of the details of my relationship with Marge prior to our marriage are now fuzzy in my mind, I do recall that we both felt strongly that this was the right thing to do. We recognized that dealing with step-children would not be easy and issues with ex-spouses would present many problems. Still, the positives seemed to outweigh the negatives. After about two years of being together, we decided to tie the knot. We were married in a large Methodist church where we had attended many excellent music programs. We had a short honeymoon in the Catskill Mountains. Nothing of great consequence occurred - there weren't any new sex games or exciting activities to try. Or so I thought!

A New Toy

Shortly after our marriage, it became obvious to me that Marge's sexual appetite was much stronger than mine. She could easily have two or three orgasms a day and still want more. Since I could not satisfy an appetite of that degree, I decided to get her a six-inch, penis-shaped, plastic vibrator. She loved it! She never had one before because it was too embarrassing to go to a sex toy shop - plus, they weren't that readily available in the seventies. At any rate, the combination of me and the vibrator apparently satisfied her libido, so things were progressing quite nicely.

But there were more games to play!

$\mathcal{T}$he $\mathcal{C}$ouples $\mathcal{E}$ncounter

One of the men I worked with was a physicist named Dennis who was married to a somewhat plump but attractive woman named Patty. They both felt their marriage needed some new excitement and were looking for ways to satisfy this craving. One evening, the four of us decided to go out for a dinner of steamed crabs. The seasoning the crabs were cooked with always produced a huge thirst that was nicely satisfied with a large pitcher of beer. We were all feeling a little tipsy when we decided to go to Marge's townhouse for snacks and after dinner drinks. Somehow, we got on the subject of Marge's open-heart surgery which she had prior to our marriage. The surgery left a large T-shaped scar on her chest. Dennis and Patty were curious to see the scar and convinced Marge to lower the top of her dress. When she did this, it naturally revealed her large, well-shaped breasts. I found this very exciting and went over to fondle them in full view of our guests. Patty decided to get into the act by lowering the top of her dress also. So, there we were - two gals with their breasts exposed and two horny guys not sure what to do next. We finally did some dancing to recorded music. I remember giving some serious thought to reaching over to fondle Patty - but wasn't sure if this would be going too far. When the music stopped, I sat down next to Marge, and then came a big surprise. Marge reached down, unzipped my pants, and proceeded to pull out my fully erect penis. I assumed that she was going to give me oral sex - which was a frequent habit of hers. But I wasn't ready for this type of exhibition, so I zipped up my pants and took Marge to our upstairs bedroom. The sex was very hot and quick! When we went back downstairs, Dennis and Patty were sitting on the couch both fully dressed. I'm not sure what went on while we were gone but I would be very surprised if they were just kissing. Strangely, we never discussed with them what took place that night despite the fact that we got together quite frequently for biking, sailing, etc. It was like it never happened!

The Beginning of The End

During the first few years of our marriage, the situation with Marge and me went quite smoothly. We took two trips to Mexico - one to visit the Mayan ruins, and one to attend her son's high school graduation in Mexico City. We also went to monthly meetings of the Spiritual Enlightenment Fellowship. We were both interested in the topics this organization dealt with including spiritualism and faith healing. We also attended numerous classes and workshops that concentrated on topics such as self-awareness and Gestalt psychology. In general, we very much enjoyed each other's company and openly professed our love for one another. However, things were about to change. My girls were now in their early teens and, although they were both good students and excellent athletes, they were getting more involved in drugs, alcohol and sex. Their mother, Alice, was working full time as a nurse in a local prison facility. She frequently worked night shifts which gave the girls ample opportunity to engage in wild parties. Alice started calling me again at Marge's place threatening to make me take full custody of the kids. Only this time, she sounded much more serious than before. I discussed the situation with Marge to see what options might be feasible. I told her that if my girls came to live with us, I would buy a larger house and even hire a maid to take care of the housework and cooking. Marge was still working as an EKG technician at a local hospital. I also told her she could quit her job and go to school full time to get her bachelor's degree. The other option would be to make my girls Wards of the State. Friends of mine who worked in this field said that this would be a disastrous mistake.

Marge's two girls who lived with us were also teen-agers at this point in time. In general, they were both well-behaved kids who Marge felt would be very negatively impacted if we all tried to live together. I frankly didn't know what to do if Alice carried through on her threat. This very stressful situation produced serious strains on my marriage to Marge. As I later learned, she secretly started to see a psychiatrist to deal with her depression. Our sex life which had been fun and playful was now becoming much less frequent and enjoyable. As a result, both of us were often using masturbation as a sexual outlet - not a good sign for a healthy marriage!

One event that reflected poor judgment on my part had to do with a diary that her older daughter, Peggy, was keeping. Peggy was an attractive teenager who was in high school and starting to date. Marge was convinced that Peggy would not get involved sexually until she was much older and wiser. She was apparently convinced that if my girls lived with us, Peggy would be unduly influenced by their wild behavior. I had my doubts that she was as pure and innocent as Marge believed. So, when the opportunity presented itself, I read a portion of her diary that revealed that she was indeed engaging in sex play with her boyfriend. I felt somewhat vindicated and shared this information with Marge. Big mistake! She was furious with me for violating Peggy's privacy. It was probably the biggest turning point in our relationship. Things were never the same after that.

A Tearful Goodbye

Due to the serious problems Marge and I were having, we both felt our only hope was to get marriage counseling. Unfortunately, the sessions were not very productive and seemed to aggravate the situation. After a few meetings with the counselor, we abandoned this approach. Shortly thereafter, we made an honest attempt to voice our feelings about how we truly felt regarding each other. I finally got up the courage to ask her - "Do you still love me?" Marge refused to answer which I took to mean that she didn't. That was the final blow. I planned to move out the next day. I felt bad our marriage had gotten to this point, but couldn't see any other viable option. I still had strong feelings for her, but couldn't live with this situation if they were not reciprocated. The next day, I was loading the car with my luggage when Marge returned from work. After she saw I was really leaving, she started to cry. That saddened me but I felt the die had been cast and a separation was the next step.

*L*essons *L*earned from *M*y *S*econd *M*arriage

There were several lessons that I learned from my five-year relationship with Marge:

1. Getting involved sexually with one's estranged spouse is a recipe for trouble, particularly if you are already romantically committed to another person. If this does happen, however, be truthful about it with your new mate. Harboring secrets of this nature does not bode well for the relationship. Let the cards fall where they may.

2. The risky games that Marge and I engaged in were fun and exciting at the time. However, I would never recommend this type of behavior now because of the potential danger associated with it - particularly in this day and age when you have so many crazies out there.

3. When we decided to marry, I felt fully confident it would be a harmonious lifetime relationship. So what went wrong? What I didn't expect and what eventually proved to be the decisive factor in the failure of our marriage was step-children. When it became clear I might have to take full custody of my girls, Marge simply could not cope with that possibility. The love she had for her own children was stronger

than her love for me. I simply didn't appreciate that fact until it was too late. Naïve again! So, it was back to the trials and tribulations of a single life.

PART SEVEN

My Commune Experience

$\mathcal{I}$ntroduction

I separated from Marge in the fall of 1977. Rather than moving back to my condo where I would be living alone, I decided it would be better for me to go to a commune-like retreat center called Kona where I had previously attended many classes and workshops. The following stories describe some of the experiences that occurred during my one-year stay.

*M*oving to *K*ona

Kona was an interesting place to live. Although it wasn't a true commune in the strict sense of the word, it had many features of that type of community. Fortunately, it was no longer a haven for drug-addicted hippies as it had been some years earlier. The staff that worked at Kona were largely professionals who were competent and took their responsibilities seriously. As I mentioned earlier, it was also known as a spiritual/educational center where Marge and I had taken many classes, workshops, and weekend retreats. There was an interesting mix of people that lived and worked there - both old and young. They also had accommodations for people to live at Kona for up to one year who were undergoing some major transition in their lives such as job loss, separation, divorce, etc. Most of the people living at Kona did not have jobs outside the community. To the best of my knowledge, I was the only one that continued to work full time at my job off campus. Hence, I was an anomaly at Kona but that was okay with me.

Kona provided me with a rather small but adequate room in one of the buildings on the grounds. Everyone who lived there was expected to do their share of housekeeping duties including dining and common rooms. All in all, it was a very interesting experience that I value to this day. As for sexual activities, not much happened except for regular episodes of masturbation. There were several incidents, however, that are worth mentioning. One involved a female resident who lived in the same building where I was located. She was a short, middle-aged pretty woman who was shy and quiet. The males living in our building noticed that, on occasion, a shoe of ours would suddenly disappear - then reappear with no explanation given. We finally found the reason. Our lady friend would borrow someone's shoe to use for masturbating. She had a shoe fetish! That was a new one for me. At any rate, she seemed perfectly normal in all other ways so we just learned to ignore her strange habit. The second incident was one for the books. During my stay at Kona, I was active again in the local singles group. One of the women I met there, Nancy, was interesting because of her wit and intelligence. She was not particularly attractive and had a figure that was not all that appealing - small breasts. Nevertheless, we enjoyed each other's company and started to date occasionally. I don't think we had the right chemistry to turn me on sexually. She was intrigued by Kona and enjoyed coming over to participate in some of the classes. One evening, we ended up going to my room where it became clear that Nancy wanted more than a platonic relationship. I explained to her that having sex in my room was not a good idea since the walls were paper thin plus the bed squeaked! We took my sleeping bag over to a small building called a Meditation Hut. It should be noted that this occurred in the middle of winter and the hut was not heated. We both got naked and crawled into the sleeping bag. I guess it was a combination of the cold and our lack of sexual chemistry because I was incapable of achieving an erection. Not wanting the evening to be a total loss, I tried to give her oral sex. It must've been a comical scene to see me struggle to get in the right position. The bottom line - nothing worked. So much for sex at Kona!

Early in my stay at Kona, I got together with Marge on a few occasions. On one of these occasions, we went out somewhere for a bite of supper. When we returned to her place, it became obvious that she didn't want me to come into her house. Instead, knowing that I was interested in some sex play, she proceeded to give me oral sex in the front seat of the car. After I came, I tried to give her some manual stimulation between her legs. Strangely, she asked me to stop because she was somewhat incontinent. What was that all about? I'll never know. We had a few other dates including a perfunctory exchange of Christmas presents, but it was obvious to me there was no desire on her part for a sincere reconciliation. I heard through the grapevine that Marge had started to date someone from the Unitarian church we had previously attended. This created some pangs of jealousy for me since I didn't expect her to abandon our relationship so quickly. On several evenings, I would drive over to her place and circle around the block hoping to see firsthand if there were any signs of her new paramour. Apparently, someone in the neighborhood recognized my car and told Marge that I was stalking her. When she called me with this news, I naturally denied it and said emphatically that someone was just making up stories. It's rather amazing to me how strangely rational people can act when they are going through a marriage separation. The bottom line to all of this was the realization that the marriage was truly over and I needed to move on to new relationships.

A few other interesting things happened while I was at Kona. At one of the weekend workshops, I met a woman who told me she was a writer of romantic fiction novels. This struck me as a possible dating opportunity. Earlier, I had taken a class at Kona on couple's massage. So, I asked her if she would be interested in some bodily manipulation. Reluctantly, she agreed to let me massage her feet but only if she could keep her socks on! I did my best, but it quickly became obvious this relationship was going nowhere. I later learned she became a well-known author of a plethora of romantic novels. Perhaps she was gay. I never knew because she did not come back to Kona. So, the quest for a new relationship continued.

There was a woman named Pat who came to Kona quite frequently. She was slight in stature and attractive. She was also bright and had a PhD in psychology. I asked her out to dinner at one of the better restaurants in the area. She agreed and so we had a very pleasant meal complete with drinks. As is usually the case after consuming a fair amount of alcohol, the conversation became more open and personal. I made it clear that I hoped we would end the evening on a romantic note. She then said to me with no hesitation - "Don't you know that I'm gay!" I really had no clue that she was a lesbian. But, in my naive way, I thought that she just hadn't met the right guy. After we got back to Kona that evening, I decided to pay her a visit. I knocked and knocked on her door and guess what. She never answered probably knowing full well that it was me hoping to get into her panties. So, the quest started anew.

There were stories circulating on the Kona campus that some of the younger staff members smoked pot regularly. I had never experienced marijuana, so I was curious to see what made it so great. Plus, I had also heard that when people got high on pot, they were more open to sexual play. One night, I went to a pot party. Surprisingly, after smoking a couple of joints, I felt nothing at all. They then passed around a pipe and that didn't do anything for me either. Finally, they suggested a technique where smoke is blown directly into the lungs. That did it. Colors became vivid and I was ready to enjoy a nice high. Suddenly, I developed a serious heart arrhythmia that scared the hell out of me. I felt death was imminent and no one was aware of my problem because they were all stoned! Finally, someone in the group recognized my plight and took me outside to get some fresh air. The most troubling part of this experience was the inability to know whether it was really happening or whether I was just dreaming. It was, without a doubt, the worst experience of my life. I later told people that if they ever needed someone to speak out against the use of mind-altering drugs, I was their man!

A New Life-Changing Experience

Kona provided many classes and workshops that dealt with self-discovery and letting it all hang out. At one of these weekend workshops, one was encouraged to individually go to the middle of mats that were placed over the entire floor. Once out there, you were instructed to undergo a series of deep-breathing exercises and then express whatever feelings come to mind regardless of how personal they might be. Most of the people who attended workshops of this type were single adults who were divorced, widowed, or involved in unhappy marriages. I was amazed at the stories that were revealed to a room full of strangers. Some of these stories had a strong sexual component that would shock many people. I felt this technique would not work with me. Surprisingly, when it was my turn, I talked freely about my past failed relationships and how they affected me. My session lasted more than two hours. Emotionally drained, I went back to the group circle feeling greatly relieved.

One of the women who attended this workshop intrigued me. She was short, attractive, and had an outgoing personality. Her name was Sarah. She was divorced and had two pre-teen children living with her. When we met, it was obvious she wanted to have some sort of dating arrangement. I made it clear to her that a monogamous relationship was of no interest to me at this point in my life. That seemed to be acceptable to her, so Sarah started coming to Kona on a regular basis. We would do things together, but basically the relationship remained platonic.

Jane the Social Worker

Shortly after meeting Sarah, I met another woman who was attending a class at Kona. Her name was Jane and she was employed as a social worker. She also had two pre-teen children living with her. Her story was tragic because of the way her former husband died. They were having marital problems that led to a separation. Apparently, he was very depressed and would call frequently to talk to Jane and the children. On one occasion, while still on the phone, he shot himself in the head and died instantly. The shock of this experience left Jane in a fragile state. She appeared to be lonely and in dire need of some male companionship. Jane, who was reasonably attractive with a fair figure, made it clear very quickly that she was anxious for more than just kissing. The heavy petting that we engaged in on the living room couch was usually done after her kids had gone to bed. She didn't want to have sex in the bedroom because of her concern that they would hear us. So, we ended up having intercourse on the living room floor. Unfortunately, this caused me to get carpet burns on my knees and elbows! She also was receptive to receiving oral sex which I was more than happy to provide. This was a new experience for Jane that she really enjoyed. However, this story has a sad end. To make intercourse more comfortable for me, she purchased a new bed and was anxious to give it a trial run. In the meantime, my relationship with Sarah had developed to the point where we were having sex on a regular basis. When I told Jane about this, she was greatly shocked and hurt. I learned rather quickly that when you have sex with someone, the idea of a free and open relationship doesn't work well. I felt sorry for Jane, but also needed to be honest with her. When the time came to say goodbye, I gave Jane a wood carving present. Without my knowledge, she returned the gift to my room at Kona. We never spoke again!

Lessons Learned at Kona

The first lesson I learned while living at Kona was the importance of having a facility of this type for people who are going through a difficult time in their lives. This is particularly true for those who have recently lost a spouse or partner because of death or divorce. Loneliness is a serious problem that can be significantly alleviated if there is an opportunity to openly discuss personal issues in a warm, caring, and accepting way. Living at Kona provided such an environment for me. However, it was also important that living there was limited to one year so one didn't become too dependent on this lifestyle.

The second lesson I learned at Kona was the value of living with people with whom you also do chores and share meals. To a significant degree, they become your extended family.

The third Kona lesson concerns the issue of being with people from all walks of life including those harboring sexual fetishes. This considerably broadened my perspective of life in general and challenged my ability to accept other people's idiosyncrasies.

PART EIGHT

Living Together

*I*ntroduction

In 1978, I left Kona and moved back to my condo. I was now in a monogamous relationship with Sarah. Due to the relatively large distance between my condo and Sarah's house, I was spending most weekends at her place. This part-time living together arrangement lasted for approximately four years. Part eight describes the tumultuous nature of this relationship.

The Sarah Story

When the affair with Jane ended, I began to spend more time with Sarah. I was attracted to her for several reasons. First, she was attractive and had a decent figure. Second, Sarah was very bright (she was a member of MENSA) and used her talents with boldness and aggressiveness. Third, she was great as a sex partner and made no bones about wanting to satisfy her lust in a variety of ways. Many of our sexual adventures occurred in places such as public parking lots, in front of hotel room windows with the drapes pulled back, etc. We both enjoyed the risk element!

I was now spending weekends at Sarah's house despite the fact that she had two pre-teen children living with her. The kids didn't seem to mind that we slept together on these weekends. On one occasion, one of them walked into her bedroom while we were at it hot and heavy. A bit embarrassing to say the least, but it didn't create any problems that I was aware of. Sarah also introduced me to a new activity that I really learned to enjoy, namely, square dancing. We joined the local square dance club and spent many evenings with this new activity. Sarah was also a member of a local Presbyterian church that she and her kids attended regularly. I would go with them and found the members of the church, including the pastor, to be very warm and welcoming. Somewhat surprising since it had to be rather obvious to all concerned that we were not married but living together on weekends.

My situation with Sarah was unusual in many ways. Early on, I had no interest in a monogamous relationship. I met several women during my stay at Kona that looked like good dating prospects. Sarah became very upset when I told her about my intentions. She burst into tears and pleaded with me to change my mind. So, largely to placate her, I agreed to not pursue these dating possibilities. Sarah seemed satisfied and was happy to continue our weekend rendezvous.

Surprisingly, the first year of our relationship went very smoothly. There were no significant disagreements or arguments that I can recall during this time. The only fly in the ointment that became very distressing for Sarah were her experiences of harassment from her ex-husband who had remarried and lived in the area. These threats became more frequent and menacing with time. On one occasion, she received a phone message that her ex had planted a bomb in her house. She called the police who came with a bomb-sniffing dog but found no evidence of foul play. Needless to say, these threats made me rather nervous when I would spend nights at her place. Some of them were so bizarre that I began to question whether they were figments of her imagination. I even got to the point where I enlisted the aid of a few of my co-workers to monitor her ex's activities including a visit to his house where he was given a warning to cease and desist his harassment of Sarah. Naturally, he denied all of these allegations and ordered us to leave. The bottom line is that we never could obtain positive proof that Sarah's claims had any merit. This went on for years!

$\mathcal{M}$ore $\mathcal{S}$ex $\mathcal{S}$tories

One of the main reasons that I stayed in my relationship with Sarah was because of the very exciting and pleasurable sex experiences that we had. Here are just a few examples.

Before I met Sarah, she told me of an episode that occurred at a square dance. Normally, women who participate wear pantaloons under their dresses. The net result is that when they are twirled the pantaloons are exposed. However, there's nothing sexy about it since they come down to about mid-thigh. On one occasion, Sarah wore nothing under her dress. When she twirled, some of the dancers would get quite a view! How daring I thought - my kind of gal.

Another incident took place when we went on a bus trip with people who were members of the local singles group. On this excursion, there was a lot of alcohol consumed. Everyone seemed to be in a playful mood. Sarah and I had more than our share to drink so inhibitions went out the window. At one point, she went to the back of the bus and sat on a guy to give him a lap dance. He returned the favor by running his hands over her breasts. It was a bold move that those nearby could hardly miss. I couldn't see any of this sex play so she provided me with all the details after returning to her seat. I was hot to trot! Unfortunately, Sarah was too drunk to do much of anything. I practically had to carry her off the bus and into our room.

The next day was different. It started out with a visit to the hotel hot tub. One of the women in the tub wore a white bathing suit that became quite transparent when it got wet. Her breasts and crotch became obvious - we found that to be arousing! Later that evening, with our sexual appetites stimulated, a group of us got dressed for bed and started frolicking in one of the hotel bedrooms. I was wearing a bathrobe with nothing underneath. Sarah wore skimpy pajamas that left little to the imagination. Several of us jumped into bed with the room lights turned off. Not sure where this was going to lead, I was rather nervous. My hands were cold and clammy, but I decided to reach out for another body anyway. Big mistake! The woman I was trying to fondle yelled out - "Your hands are freezing." That ended it for me. When the lights came back on, Sarah pulled my robe up for all to see my bare butt. Someone managed to take a picture of me in that position. It became one of our prized possessions. But that's not all. After my hands warmed up, I decided to give Sarah a massage that started with the abdomen. With several people looking on, I proceeded to work my hands southward and lowered her pajamas to the point of showing some pubic hair. Everyone was cheering us on. Sarah reached under my robe and fondled me. That gave an observing couple sufficient reason to get under the sheets and make out. We went back to our room and did the same.

Early in our relationship, Sarah told me about an incident that occurred during one of her out of town speaking engagements. At an evening banquet, she found herself seated between two men whom she quickly befriended. After a bit of small talk, the topic turned to the subject of sex. She decided to make the conversation more interesting by reaching under the table and placing her hands on their thighs. She then proceeded to fondle them much to their amazement and delight. As you might expect, when the banquet was over, both guys wanted to pursue this teasing by accompanying Sarah to her hotel room. She claims they took turns having fun which included intercourse, fellatio, and anal sex.

Apparently, this went on for hours. Surprisingly, no one seemed worried about sexually transmitted diseases. Herpes was of some concern, but AIDS was relatively unknown at this point in time. Pregnancy was also not an issue - Sarah had a tubal ligation some years earlier. The next day, she was somewhat sore from all this nocturnal activity. After Sarah returned home, we restrained our sexual activities for a few days. Nevertheless, she felt I would enjoy hearing about her orgy. She was so right even though I didn't know how much of the story was really true or how much was made up to amuse me. At that point in time, I really didn't care - it was still fun and stimulating!

*O*ur *O*nly *A*ttempt at *S*winging

After a couple of years had gone by, Sarah and I decided it would be exciting to consider swinging with another couple. We had seen articles in some of the local publications which included men seeking women, women seeking men, etc. One notice that caught our attention was from a couple who wanted to explore the possibility of swapping partners if all concerned were mutually agreeable. They didn't state their ages or mention photographs, but rather suggested a meeting at a bar where, over drinks, we could size each other up and talk about possible future arrangements. So we gave this couple a call and arranged to meet them at a local lounge that was conveniently located for all of us. Naturally, we were quite anxious about this type of arrangement. We didn't know what to expect, but thought - what the heck - let's give it a shot! I can't remember how we planned to recognize each other. But whatever the plan, we had no trouble meeting them when we got to the lounge. As it turned out, they were a reasonably attractive couple but considerably younger in age. They appeared to be quite nervous about what we were doing and confessed this was also their first experience. We found a booth for four in a relatively quiet location in the lounge and quickly had a drink or two. Feeling a bit more relaxed, we engaged in some small talk before finally getting to the subject of sex. As it turned out, they were not that keen on exchanging partners. Rather, they felt it might be exciting to engage in sex play with all four of us in the same room. We said we would think about it and get back to them. We never did and they didn't call us either. So much for swinging!

The End of The Sarah Saga

My relationship with Sarah lasted for approximately four years. After the first year, we started to have arguments that sometimes had her screaming at me. When these events occurred, I would leave and go back to my condo. Later in the week, she would call and apologize and plead for me to come back. We decided that if our relationship had any chance of succeeding, we would need to seek professional help. So we did. Over the course of two years, we went to several marriage counselors - all to no avail. Further complicating our problems were Sarah's claims that her ex-husband was continuing to harass and threaten her. It finally got to the point where we decided to seek the help of a psychiatrist who had the reputation of being the best marriage counselor in the area. For six months, we saw this individual on a weekly basis. That didn't work either! I finally came to the conclusion there was no hope for us. At one of our sessions with the psychiatrist, I expressed my thoughts about ending the relationship. The psychiatrist acted very surprised by this revelation. He asked me how he could have handled the situation differently. I told him he was worried about landscaping issues when in fact, the house was burning down. I don't think he appreciated that assessment, but finally realized that I was serious and not about to change my mind. I saw Sarah one more time after that session. I went to her place to pick up some of my things. She asked me if was interested in renewing our relationship. When I told her no, she said she was going to date an editor who was handling a book which she had just co-authored. I later learned that this book became a best seller and is still in demand to this day. Sometime later, I received a call from Sarah asking me if I could give her the name of a good financial planner. Obviously, the royalties from the book were paying her handsomely. I never heard from her again!

Lessons Learned from My Living-Together Relationship

My four-year relationship with Sarah was very different from anything else I experienced. The reasons I say this are:

1. We never discussed love for one another despite the fact that we lived together on weekends during most of this time.
2. The possibility of eventually getting engaged and/or married was never considered.
3. The factors that drew me to Sarah such as her attractiveness, brightness, and aggressiveness, were eventually offset by what I felt were serious personality problems. I could no longer believe all of the stories that she claimed were being perpetrated by her ex-husband.
4. I could not see any long-term future for our relationship. She was not the woman I wanted to be with for the rest of my life.

So what lessons did I learn from all of this? Several come to mind. First, a living-together relationship is no guarantee that one will be able to make the necessary adjustments for a happy, stable lifetime commitment. When arguments arose, I would escape to my condo until tempers cooled down - which sometimes lasted for days. Not a realistic technique for married couples.

Second, professional counseling simply didn't work despite many attempts to try this approach. Third, as in my previous marriage to Marge, step-children became an issue. Only this time, the problem was with Sarah and her teen-age son. Although this didn't affect me directly, it became a major problem for Sarah requiring much of her time and energy.

PART NINE

Dating Again

$\mathcal{I}$ntroduction

When my relationship with Sarah ended in 1983, I was fifty-three years old and still looking for a suitable female partner for companionship - and sex if the chemistry was right. Hence, I dated a number of women during the next year. The stories that follow in Part Nine describe these relationships - both the good and the bad!

Back to The Dating Game

After my four-year saga with Sarah came to an end, I decided to start dating again. However, this time I was determined to avoid monogamous relationships despite the fact that many women are uncomfortable with any other type of arrangement. When I attended my first event at the local singles group, I was pleasantly surprised by the attractive women that were seemingly available.

One of these, a woman named Toby, was particularly interesting for a number of reasons. First, she was nice looking with a decent figure. Second, she was a writer who had published several books. Third, she struck me as a person who was bright and had a wide range of interests. Toby told me she was divorced and had a pre-teen daughter who lived with her. That concerned me but I figured it was worth a try. My first visit to her place quickly changed my mind. Her daughter clearly did not appreciate her mother dating and made it abundantly clear she didn't like me. So that ended our relationship. I never even got a kiss from Toby!

Strangely, I met another woman shortly thereafter who was also named Toby. What amazed me about Toby number two was her very affectionate behavior. She constantly wanted to hold hands and snuggle which was endearing. I assumed she would be good in bed. She had a strange habit, however. When we were at her place, doing some passionate kissing and petting on her living room couch, she insisted on keeping the drapes open. She didn't explain why and I didn't ask. At any rate, I decided if we were going to make out, it would have to be at my condo. So the next time we got together, we went to my place where I was looking forward to great sex. I was very wrong! It was the worst sex I ever experienced. She appeared to be just going through the act to please me, but got nothing out of it for herself. So much for Toby number two!

Another Toby

And then there was Toby number three! I met her at an institute for spiritual studies located in New York State. This facility is a very interesting retreat center where a large variety of courses and workshops are offered many of which were similar to those conducted at Kona. Toby was not particularly attractive nor did she have much of a figure. However, for whatever reason, she found me interesting and wanted to be my companion a good deal of the time. That was okay with me except for one problem. Toby was married and her husband was with her at the retreat center. Apparently, they had an open marriage and were making it quite obvious they had no qualms about her affectionate behavior toward me. In several group gatherings, Toby would be sitting next to me arm-in-arm while her husband was just a few feet away. I wasn't comfortable with that sort of relationship so it was never pursued further.

Teacher Number One

Back home, other dating opportunities were starting to develop. One involved a high school teacher named Ann. She was attractive with a decent figure and had a very friendly, gregarious personality.

I liked Ann as a person and enjoyed doing things with her. However, there was a lack of sexual chemistry between us. Despite my misgivings, we ended up one night at my condo. We started out on the living room couch with kissing and petting. She was not the type to be bashful so it didn't take long before her hand was on my crouch which, to my delight, produced a good, hard erection. To make things more comfortable, we proceeded to the bedroom where we continued our sex play. Two surprises! One, Ann had no pubic hair. I didn't ask her why - whether it was Mother Nature or whether she shaved. This was my first encounter with an adult hairless pussy! The second surprise was associated with her technique for getting vaginal lubrication. Apparently, she did not produce enough in a natural way, so she used her saliva to remedy the dryness problem. Well, guess what happened. I immediately lost my erection and no amount of manual stimulation was able to bring it back. She tried to give me oral sex but that didn't work either. Ann was not particularly upset with this situation. She felt that we should just go on with things and that our sex life would improve with time. I, however, didn't think so. I felt the lack of pheromones was a significant problem that wouldn't get better. Ann became very upset with my theory and got quite angry. She later told me that soon after our failed attempt at lovemaking, she went to bed with a young man she had just met and didn't have a problem. My rebuttal was that young men probably don't need the stimulation of female pheromones. For my age, it was an important element - at least for me! At any rate, we stopped seeing each other which, in looking back, was probably the right choice for both of us.

Teacher Number Two

During the time I was dating Ann, I was also active in square and round dancing with another teacher named Mary. Our relationship was purely platonic - just dancing and nothing more! I liked Mary as a person and enjoyed her company. She was pretty but on the heavy side. However, that was not important to me because I was into this relationship strictly for dancing. There was a sad side to the story as I later learned. Mary was a widow who lived with two pre-teen sons and her father. The tragic part was how her husband died. A few years earlier, she received a call from the police that a fire occurred in a movie theater and her husband was a fatality. Even more shocking was that this theater was well-known as a Mecca for homosexuals. Mary had no idea that her husband was gay. Apparently, he kept it a secret throughout their marriage. I felt sorry for her to have gone through such a traumatic experience. Fortunately, she appeared to have adjusted well to the situation and was quite happy and content.

One night, a surprising thing happened in our

relationship. While we were getting instructions on a new round-dance step, Mary was standing beside me closer than usual. I could feel her breast rubbing against my arm. I realized this was not an accidental maneuver since it continued throughout the lesson. When I took her home that evening, she asked me to come in for a nightcap. After a drink or two, inhibitions were diminished and we quickly found ourselves in her bedroom. Since it was late, we presumed her father and sons were asleep. When we got in bed, I lost my erection! So, not wanting to be a disappointment, I put my head between her legs. Mary had never experienced cunnilingus and appeared to enjoy it. We then had intercourse - the pheromones were now working! I tried to make it clear to Mary that having sex with her should not be taken as a sign that I was interested in having a serious, monogamous relationship. Also, her father wanted to know if we were planning to get married. Apparently, he was not asleep as we had presumed! This worried us, so we decided to continue as friends but not lovers.

Lessons Learned from Dating Again

My second round of dating involved issues that were very similar to those I encountered five years earlier.

First and foremost was the confirmation of my original belief that dating in the singles world can be a stressful and unsatisfying experience. As I stated before, getting involved with more than one person at the same time can create serious problems particularly if the parties know one another.

Regarding singles sex, not too much changed in this department. Most of the women I met were still not interested in casual sex. Instead, as before, they were looking for partners who would commit to a monogamous relationship. The lesson I learned here was not to get sexually involved with someone unless you are seriously interested in pursuing such an arrangement. If the relationship progresses to the point where there are thoughts of marriage, you need to know that person intimately. This includes one's views on sex, children, religion, politics and money matters. It is critical that both parties be frank and honest. Deception in these areas will create problems that will be very difficult to cope with later.

In my case, I didn't follow this advice. Something that later came back to haunt me. Naive again! This leads me to the story of Barbara which ended my dating experiences.

$\mathscr{B}$arbara $\mathscr{E}$nters the $\mathscr{P}$icture

When the relationships with the two teachers came to an end, I decided to begin anew in my quest for a suitable partner by revisiting the local singles group. At one of these gatherings, there was an attractive woman with a nice figure. She had short brown hair, large blue eyes, rosy cheeks, amd wore make-up that enhanced her appearance in a tasteful way. She was also of medium height and had an athletic build - she exuded the picture of good health. When I introduced myself, it quickly became clear that she had a gregarious personality and was very direct and straightforward. Those features greatly appealed to me. For example, shortly after we started conversing, she asked me my age. I later learned that she didn't want to get involved with a younger man. As it turned out, I was about five years older so that part looked promising. Her name was Barbara and, much to my surprise, was also a high school teacher. She was a divorcee, had been married twice before, and had three children one of whom still lived with her. Peter was about eight years old. The idea of getting seriously involved with a person who was raising a young child caused me to have a number of doubts; particularly after the problems I had in my marriage to Marge. However, Peter was bright and friendly. He appeared to be pleased with the fact that his mother was dating.

On one of our first dates, we ended the evening by

going to Barbara's modest house where we did some kissing and light petting on the living room couch. Then something happened that surprised me. "Lay on me," she said with no hesitation. We were both fully clothed so I didn't quite understand what she had in mind. Nevertheless, I did what she requested and wondered what would come next. As it turned out, she didn't want to go any further because of the possibility that Peter might walk in on us. The evening ended with some kisses but with the promise of more to come.

On our next date, we decided to go to my condo where we had a cocktail or two. Barbara then suggested we head for the bedroom where she quickly shed her clothes. Somewhat reluctantly, I followed suit but was concerned her aggressive approach to sex might cause me to have an erection problem. However, that was not the case at all. With a minimum of foreplay, I entered her waiting pussy and came quickly much to my delight. Incidentally, no condom was used because there wasn't a need for one as far as pregnancy was concerned. We simply didn't worry about sexually transmitted diseases - I'm not sure why. Then something happened that was a first for me. Barbara wanted to have a second round of intercourse - just minutes after our first! Surprisingly, I was able to achieve another erection quickly and we went at it again. She gave every indication of now being sexually satisfied which made me feel good. I didn't think it was possible for me to come twice in a row and attributed this to good pheromones. Later, I noticed she had dug her fingernails into my back which left a few scratches. A mark of true passion I thought!

This first encounter opened the door to a whole series of sexual experiences with Barbara. Most took place at my condo although several were at her house when Peter was not home. One of these that I will never forget occurred in her family room. We were both naked and in a standing position. I put my hands on her well-shaped butt and lifted her up high enough for intercourse. We came quickly - probably partly due to the novelty of having sex in this manner. However, there was a problem with this technique since it put quite a strain on my back - an issue that lasts to this day! We never tried it again.

There were other factors in our relationship that drew us closer together. Besides being attractive, Barbara was very loving. She was also very much into oral sex - both giving and receiving. So was I. With all of these plus factors going for us, we started to discuss the possibility of marriage.

Things Get Serious

When we talked about the pros and cons of marriage, there were several serious issues that needed to be considered. First was the fact that Barbara was a devout Roman Catholic who attended mass every week. I, on the other hand, was a Unitarian and had been active with this organization for over thirty years. Nevertheless, I was always attracted to the rituals and pageantry associated with Catholic services. When we discussed the situation with a priest, he said that he did not see a problem with our getting married in a civil ceremony despite the fact that I was never baptized and did not consider myself to be a Christian. We decided to attend both services every week. The priest said that if we ever wanted to get married in the Roman Catholic Church, we would have to get our prior marriages annulled - a long, expensive, and emotionally painful process!

A second factor had to do with Peter. Barbara was adamant that he attend Catholic grade and high schools because of her lack of trust in the public system despite the fact that she was a special education teacher in a public high school. This requirement would involve considerable expense that I would have to largely subsidize.

Third, there was the question of where we would live. My one-bedroom condo was not large enough for the three of us. Her house also lacked many of the amenities that we felt were important such as a private bathroom for Peter, a fireplace, etc.

Finally, there was the question of sexual compatibility. As we got to know one another better, it became clear that Barbara had many previous sexual experiences - both male and female. Hence, she was very good in this department. I enjoyed hearing about her past escapades and found them to be exciting rather than a turnoff. So, all in all, it appeared that we were sexually well suited for each other. A major plus factor for a possible marriage.

PART TEN

My Third Marriage

$\mathcal{I}$ntroduction

Barbara and I were married in the spring of 1984. Like most marriages, it had its ups and downs. Initially, the ups outnumbered the downs. However, as time passed, the opposite was true. During the final months of our marriage, which lasted eight years, the situation with Barbara became very difficult and contentious; one of the worst experiences of my life! Hopefully, the following stories will enable the reader to get some insight into this third marriage "train wreck".

The Decision is Made

After considering all the pros and cons of marriage, we decided to proceed with a civil ceremony while simultaneously applying for annulments. The wedding took place within six months of our first meeting. One might wonder why we didn't wait for a longer period of time in order to get to know each other better. Living together was not acceptable to Barbara due to her religious beliefs and because of the effect it might have on Peter. My gut feeling was that we could make marriage work.

We also decided to buy a new three-bedroom townhouse on one of the lakes in the area. This provided us with ample space and privacy. It even had a functional fireplace in the lower level. This cozy location provided plenty of opportunity for sex on the carpeted floor when we felt Peter was upstairs sleeping. On at least one occasion, however, he came down during one of our love-making sessions. We quickly covered ourselves with a blanket but it had to be obvious to Peter what was going on. I felt he resented the affection that Barbara was showing me. It was clearly a different world for him than when he was his mother's prime focus. He also resented the fact that we purchased the town house without consulting him first. I was surprised that he felt we needed his okay for such a decision. Trouble was brewing on the horizon!

Trying to Make Things Better

Sensing there were going to be serious problems between Barbara, Peter and myself, a number of things were done to help remedy the situation.

First, Peter was enrolled in a Catholic grade school associated with Barbara's church. It was expensive, but affordable since both of us were working.

Second, I tried my best to assist Peter with his schoolwork including an ambitious science fair project. This helped somewhat in my relationship with him, but not to the extent I had hoped.

Third, living on the shores of a lake, I bought a small sailboat that could accommodate all of us. This turned out to be a smart move that even Peter enjoyed.

Fourth, Barbara and I decided to undertake a do-it-yourself patio project. This was also a successful undertaking particularly since Peter pitched in to help. Barbara felt this was one of the best things that happened in our family relationship. I hoped she was right but had my doubts.

Another major attempt to help my relationship with Peter involved supporting his interest in athletics. He started participating in a number of sports activities including tennis, lacrosse, and wrestling. He started playing these games when he was still in grade school. He joined a wrestling club that had daily practice sessions plus many matches with neighboring teams. Naturally, this involved taking him to the events, watching him compete, and bringing him home. This went on for several years and involved a large amount of time and expense on our part. I didn't resent doing this since sports in general were a strong interest for me. I particularly liked tennis and became a fair player.

Peter, on the other hand, found tennis to be very challenging and became quite upset when he couldn't beat me. This changed as he became older and found that he could hold his own in a match. I felt this would help things between the two of us. Naive again!

Sex-The Good and The Bad

During the years that we lived in the townhouse, sex with Barbara was mostly good and frequent.

She had a flair for doing things to spice up our lives. For example, I would come home from work occasionally and find her wearing a see-through negligee. We would often engage in oral stimulation, both ways, followed by satisfying intercourse. The relationship, however, was marred by frequent arguments that would often result in our not speaking to each other for a prolonged period. I would sleep on the couch during these episodes which was upsetting. Surprisingly, after a few days went by, Barbara would become very sweet and loving and we would have great make-up sex.

Another thing she often did when we were having these arguments was to openly flirt with other men. This would usually occur at dances, parties, sporting events, and even with some of our neighbors. It drove me wild when she did this and became a major factor in the unraveling of our marriage. I've often said to myself regarding Barbara - "When she is good, she is very, very good; but when she is bad, she is horrid."

Religion Becomes an Important Factor

Barbara made it clear that she wanted us to be married in a Catholic ceremony. As stated previously, this was acceptable to the priest provided we got annulments of our previous ones. So we decided to go through with the process which took almost a year since it had to go to the Vatican for final approval. The ceremony was simple. It was held in a small chapel on the church grounds with no guests except for Peter. I thought this act would strengthen my relationship with Barbara plus have a positive influence on Peter. Naive again!

Although we went to mass regularly, I still felt no need to get baptized and become a bona fide Christian. Then, I experienced a strange and totally unexpected event. During one of the rituals held at the church called the Benediction of the Host, there was a copious amount of incense used plus the congregants sang in Latin. Suddenly, I felt the time had come for me to convert to Catholicism. This was not a rational decision. It was a mystical experience pure and simple.

Since this is a book that is based primarily on sexual experiences, I won't go into the details of my religious journey except to say that I became a devout, practicing Catholic for many years. I also experienced many mini miracles that defy any scientific explanation. This could and probably will be the subject of another book.

The Drums Fiasco

About two years after we were living in the townhouse, Peter decided that he wanted to learn to play the drums. Naturally, Barbara wanted to placate him so we ended up purchasing a complete set including cymbals. As you can imagine, when he beat on them, the noise reverberated throughout our entire house and the neighboring townhouses as well. It became clear very quickly that Barbara was not about to limit Peter's new-found activity. As a matter of fact, she encouraged him to play his drums whenever he felt in the mood. I assumed this would soon be a passing fad. Naive again! Hence, although we enjoyed living in our townhouse, it became obvious we needed to find a larger abode which would be isolated from our neighbors. I should add at this point that sex with Barbara was usually very good. That was about to change!

Paradise Found (OR SO IT SEEMED)

After more than a year of searching for a new house, we finally found one that met all of our needs. It was located on a large wooded lot and was a single-story ranch house with separate wings for three bedrooms. That enabled us to have ample privacy. It also had a separate building on the grounds that made an ideal place for Peter to practice his drums and for Barbara to do her artwork; a hobby at which she became quite proficient.

New Problems Arise

On one occasion when Barbara was working at her high school, a fight broke out between two students. Trying to be the consummate peacemaker, she attempted to separate them and managed to get hit by a blow that knocked her into a locker. According to her version, she suffered a head injury that resulted in permanent brain damage. She quit her job and applied for social security disability. After numerous visits to doctors who specialized in injuries of this type, she was awarded a lifetime disability pension. Perhaps this new source of income convinced Barbara she no longer needed me for financial stability. Unfortunately, her personality changed for the worse. Our priest also felt she was showing signs of being mentally unstable.

Another problem developed that involved using a friend's new hot tub. What started as a pleasurable experience sitting around and relaxing in the tub, turned out to be a serious matter. Shortly after this event, I developed a slight crotch infection that persisted despite my best efforts to deal with it by using over-the-counter medications. My doctor told me it was a fungus infection that probably came from the hot tub. He said it would go away by using an anti-fungal cream. I didn't say anything to Barbara about the problem which was a big mistake. There were several occasions when we had sex during this time. When I later told Barbara, she became furious and accused me of trying to give her a venereal disease. Nothing could convince her that this was not true. Her paranoid personality, however, reared its ugly head and she never changed her negative feelings towards me. Our sex life took a dramatic downturn even after the infection was gone. Fellatio was now out of the question. Intercourse became much less frequent and, when it did occur, it lacked the spice and spontaneity that we had previously enjoyed.

Although the move to the new house looked like the right thing to do, other problems developed that put a serious strain on our marriage. Again, many of these had to do with Peter. At some point in his relationship with the Catholic Church we were attending, he became very friendly with one of the staff members of the church school. This individual was rumored to be gay although no one knew for sure.

An added troubling factor involved the priest who married us. He was found to be a sexual predator and was eventually defrocked. Also, Barbara found literature in Peter's room that dealt with Satanism. All of these events greatly concerned her to the point where she made it very clear that Peter was the primary focus of her life. Our relationship was a secondary consideration. The situation became serious enough that we decided to get marriage counseling. A counselor was selected who came highly recommended and was also a practicing Catholic - something that both of us felt could be important.

We saw him weekly for several months but it didn't

work. Barbara felt he was siding with me on too many issues. It was also about this time that financial issues became a problem. For some reason that I will never understand, she suddenly withdrew a large sum of money from our jointly-owned savings account and put it into another account in her name only. When it became apparent from the bank statement, I became very angry and insisted the money be put back. Barbara argued that she felt financially insecure in our marriage and the money would eventually be returned. I did not believe her and said our marriage was in serious trouble. Both of us hired divorce attorneys and started the process of deciding who would get what after we finally split. This was a very difficult and time-consuming project that further stressed our relationship. Barbara moved to a spare bedroom and our sex life came to a halt.

The End Looms

The situation with Barbara looked hopeless. However, I still felt there might be a chance for reconciliation. Living apart but under one roof was very stressful for both of us. She anticipated I would move out and that we might start a dating relationship. This was a total surprise which made me wonder what she had in mind. One night, after a drink or two, I put my hand on her breast. She withdrew and said "It's too early for that." I attributed her reaction to indicate there might be some hope in the future. When she got "horny", masturbation was not an option. Rather, she wanted a penis in her vagina or a tongue on her clit - or both. Something I used to do frequently much to her delight. Since retirement to Florida was close, I did not move out. In the meantime, we completed the very complicated division of assets. An interesting incident occurred during this time. It was rather obvious to me that Peter was quite happy that I would be leaving. When asked why he didn't express his dislike for me before we got married, he said he knew this move would help them financially. Something I never recognized at the time - naive again!

Lessons Learned from My Third Marriage

The problems encountered in my marriage to Barbara were somewhat similar to those in my last two relationships. These include the following:

1. I was initially attracted to Barbara because of her good looks, nice figure, and her sexuality. This caused me to overlook some troubling personality traits that later proved to be very destructive to our marriage.

2. Barbara was a divorced mother raising a young child, Peter, who was a major concern to her particularly as he entered his teen-age years.

3. Although not poor, money was a significant factor in Barbara's search for a suitable mate. She was looking for someone who could make life better for her and Peter.

In reviewing these problems, I could see a pattern in my choice of mates that was quite troubling.

In addition, there were some new issues with Barbara that further stressed our marriage.

First and foremost was her obsessive need to satisfy all of Peter's wants and desires. Despite my best efforts to be a supportive stepfather, it was clear that he didn't accept me and felt I was intruding on the relationship he had with his mother.

Second, Barbara had a strong propensity to be flirtatious with other men particularly when we were dealing with our own problems. This was very upsetting and made me realize that jealousy was an issue I don't handle well.

Third, I learned over time that Barbara had no qualms about lying and cheating when it suited her needs. Near the end of our marriage, it became clear to me that she was a pathological liar.

Finally, when Barbara was granted a disability pension due to her head injury, she no longer needed me for financial support. That was the "kiss of death" for our marriage, resulting in a difficult and contentious divorce.

So what to do next? My story continues as I retire and move to Florida.

Florida Beckons

Approximately two years before our separation, we discussed the possibility of moving south after my retirement. An article about an organization based in Florida called the Senior Academy intrigued me. We made a trip to learn more about this group. I was impressed and decided this would be a great way to spend my retirement years. Hence, when it became clear that we were going our separate ways, I decided to move to Florida by myself and apply for membership in the academy. After my retirement in 1992, I gave Barbara a final hug and bade her farewell. Strangely, I still thought there might be some hope for a later reconciliation.

After getting settled in my new abode in Florida, I felt the need to undergo some psychological counseling to learn more about myself. I also wanted to explore in depth why my three previous marriages ended up on the rocks. Was I attracted to women who were the wrong type for me? Or, was there a basic problem of my own? I needed some answers before embarking on any new female relationships.

Another important issue; after we stopped sleeping in the same bed, I relied solely on masturbation to satisfy my sexual appetite. As a practicing Catholic at the time, I went to confession on a regular basis. The Roman

Catholic Church considers masturbation to be a sin. It also considers sex outside of marriage to be a sin. Which was worse? Celibacy was not an option for me. So what to do? At age sixty-two, time was of the essence!

$\mathscr{P}$rogress is $\mathscr{M}$ade

After doing considerable soul searching, I decided to see a psychologist who did personal counseling and was known for his Christian values. These sessions occurred once a week for several months and involved taking a battery of tests designed to evaluate many aspects of one's personality, abilities, and interests. They were very helpful and gave my ego a considerable boost! In addition to counseling, attending prayer meetings at a Catholic retreat center became a regular practice. These sessions, combined with worship at a local church, satisfied my spiritual needs. However, I did not want to face my senior years living by myself. I wanted a compatible partner who had similar interests and values. Casual dating was no longer of interest even if it provided sexual possibilities.

Masturbation, despite producing some feelings of guilt, was adequate for the time being.

$\mathscr{D}$onna $\mathscr{E}$nters $\mathscr{T}$he $\mathscr{P}$icture

After being accepted as a member of the Senior Academy, I met a woman who worked for this organization as the program administrator. She handled the paperwork associated with applicants and was familiar with my situation although my background information indicated that I was still married. Her name was Donna. She was attractive with an engaging smile that was appealing to everyone. She wore her salt and pepper hair in a bun which gave her a prim and proper appearance. Donna was exceptionally well-groomed and used make up to enhance her dark-brown eyes and shapely lips. Figure wise, she was petite with a nicely-shaped body, particularly in the boob department. Another outstanding feature that Donna possessed was her genuine interest when dealing with others. She was a touchy-feely person who frequently reached out to physically interact with both men and women. Donna also had a true gift of expressing kind words, both verbally and in writing, to people with whom she interacted. Dress wise, she usually wore skirt suits to the academy that gave her a very professional appearance. Finally, and of great importance to me, was her intelligence and organizational abilities.

All of these features provided a very attractive package that I felt could be worth pursuing. My greatest concern, however, was my initial belief that Donna was too prim and proper for me - probably not my type. Nevertheless, I felt it would be worthwhile to know her better. Fortunately, there was a mutual interest in pursuing this path. We decided the best way to do this would be for me to bring my lunch to the academy and join Donna in her office during the noon hour. We closed the door so we could talk in privacy without any interruptions.

Our Pasts are Revealed

After a few of these lunch-time sessions, I learned that Donna was divorced and had one adult child who no longer lived with her. Hence, I wanted to take our relationship to the next level and asked her to have dinner with me. To my surprise, her answer was not yet because she was presently in a committed relationship with a man who was living with her. She felt dating would not be wise. However, she anticipated ending the relationship in the near future. Another important factor in our feelings towards one another had to do with Barbara. I needed to know if there was any hope of reconciliation after several months of separation. This was discussed with my counselor. He strongly suggested that I ask her this question directly. Reluctantly, I made a call and was told by Barbara she had no interest in pursuing the matter. Her quick negative response was a surprise. However, it now felt right to pursue my interest in Donna.

During our lunch-time conversations, I made it clear to her that I had a checkered past when it came to my relationships with women. I told her in considerable detail about my sexual peccadilloes. I wondered if this would be a turnoff for her. Surprisingly, it wasn't. She had been married and divorced twice and was living with her present partner. She also told me about other sexual experiences she had during her lifetime. This piqued my interest since it was now obvious that

Donna was not a "Miss Goody Two Shoes." There were several other factors that convinced me that we might have something going for us.

One had to do with our lunch-time conversations. We would hug and kiss on the lips before leaving her office. Much to my delight and embarrassment, this caused me to have an erection! By holding my briefcase in front of me, I thought Donna might not notice. Later, she told me it was obvious what was happening and was pleased with my arousal. These events convinced me there was sexual chemistry with us - probably due to Donna having an abundant supply of pheromones. Whatever the reason, that was a good sign.

A second factor was her willingness to view sex videos. These tapes were well done with attractive models. They graphically depicted a variety of intercourse positions and oral sex activities. Both of us found them stimulating.

A third factor which was important to me was her appearance. She was admired by many other men. It made me feel good that someone this appealing could be interested in me.

A fourth factor had to do with our spiritual values. Although Donna was not a Roman Catholic, she was open to attending mass and other Catholic activities. At the time, this was an important part of my life and I was pleased she was willing to share it with me.

The final factor worth mentioning concerned our family relationships. Both Donna and I had grown children who were living elsewhere. In looking back on my previous two marriages, I felt living with step-children caused serious problems that contributed significantly to the failure of these relationships. Furthermore, Donna's parents, who also lived in Florida, accepted me in spite of my past. In private, her father cautioned me to not get involved with her unless I wanted a sincere, long-term relationship. I assured him that was my intent and so it was.

PART ELEVEN

I Finally Got It Right!

Donna Makes a Move

About three months after we met, Donna decided to end the relationship with her live-in partner, Will, and move to a condo complex near the academy. I thought we could now date on a regular basis without any serious complications. Naive again! Will was very upset with Donna's leaving and began to stalk our every move. He even went so far as to call Barbara to tell her about our relationship. Surprisingly, she told him all sorts of nasty things about me including her opinion that I was only looking for short-term relationships. He promptly told Donna what Barbara had said hoping that she would drop me and return to him. Well, that didn't happen. Instead, we decided to get married as soon as possible despite the fact that it couldn't be done in a Catholic ceremony without a long and expensive annulment proceeding.

Sex Enters the Picture

One topic that hasn't been discussed yet regarding my relationship with Donna is the matter of sexual compatibility. When she moved, we finally had a safe haven for sex. Previously, I would occasionally have an erection problem during my first attempts at intercourse with a new partner. Fortunately, that wasn't the case with Donna. What amazed me was how wet Donna was between her legs. I assumed she used a lot of lubricant to make intercourse more comfortable. Later, she told me that a dryness problem prior to our meeting was of concern. Her doctor prescribed estrogen which really did the job! I never experienced anything like it. Donna was also willing to give me oral sex, but was reluctant to have me return the favor. As it turned out, oral sex was not our favorite activity. Intercourse was just fine! Another thing that surprised me was Donna's sexual appetite. During our early courting days, she was more eager to make love than I was. Probably the biggest difference in our amorous play had to do with pre-intercourse fondling. Donna liked to be caressed gently and slowly, particularly her arms, legs and back. I liked things somewhat harder and faster. She also didn't care much for having her breasts fondled and kissed; one of my favorite activities. We eventually solved most of these problems. However, it took time and patience - an important element in any marriage.

New Challenges and New Opportunities in Our Sex Life

Over the course of our twenty-five-year marriage, more challenges developed in the sex department that required new approaches. The first had to do with heart arrhythmia problems that I experienced during most of my adult life. These required that I take drugs called beta blockers. The medicines did a good job except that it became more and more difficult for me to achieve and maintain an erection. So I decided to try the "little blue pills." Initially, they worked well and we were able to have intercourse on a regular basis. Eventually, however, the pills lost their efficacy. They also started to give me headaches; so I quit. The net result was we didn't have intercourse as often. I needed more stimulation to achieve an erection. We watched a variety of adult videos which both of us enjoyed. I also liked hearing about Donna's previous sexual exploits - something she was willing to do because it brought me pleasure. Since this storytelling was not Donna's favorite activity, it was usually reserved for those times when I needed extra help.

Another difference in our lovemaking had to do with the time it took to reach a climax. Usually, my orgasm came fast. It took longer for Donna. For her to reach a climax, she found a vibrator to be a useful tool. A loud groan signaled the peak of pleasure for me. Donna, on the other hand, was quiet. It felt like I was enjoying sex more than her. However, the biggest challenges were yet to come! One of them occurred after we had been married about fifteen years. As we were having intercourse one night, Donna found she was experiencing discomfort including some vaginal bleeding. She had stopped taking estrogen some years ago because of the cancer scare issues that were being reported. As a result, she started to have some dryness issues that were now causing a serious problem when we tried to have intercourse. Going back on estrogen was never a viable option for her - a decision with which I agreed. The bottom line was that we stopped having intercourse entirely. Thus, we agreed that some new and creative ways of sex play were needed.

A Different Solution

One of the practices I used often since my teen years was masturbation. Using a sexual lubricant, I found it was possible to reach an orgasm without irritating my penis. Furthermore, much to my surprise, I could do this without having a full erection. This may not be true for most men, but it certainly worked for me. Prior to masturbating, we would engage in French kissing, massaging, and on occasion watching an adult video or describing a past sexual experience. Donna would achieve an orgasm by using the vibrator on her clit; no need for vaginal penetration. These techniques worked successfully for many years - but then a different toy came into the picture.

The New Sex Toy

It was claimed that a man could enhance his orgasm by using an anal vibrator to stimulate the prostate gland. Several of the magazines that we received described devices of this type for reasonable prices. As a surprise gift, Donna ordered one for me. When I first tried to use it, it became evident that plenty of lubricant was needed plus the ability to relax the anal sphincter muscle. Also, I found that size does matter. The second device of this type that I got had a stronger vibrator and was easier to use. However, it was simply too big in diameter. Despite many attempts, I was never able to get it past that strong muscle. At any rate, the smaller device worked well enough. It may be that the use of such a sex toy produces pleasure because of the extra stimulation it provides. Or, it may be partially psychological. At any rate, it helps me and I use it to this day.

A Final Note

In finishing my story, it would be a mistake if I didn't mention a problem that probably affects most senior citizens; namely, a decrease in sex drive that accompanies aging. In my sixties and seventies, I wanted to have sexual relief at least once a week. Most of the time, this would involve Donna. Sometimes, however, I would take care of things in the shower. In my eighties, my sex drive decreased significantly so that now, at age eighty-eight, having sexual relief every month or so is sufficient. My belief is that sex goes hand-in-hand with good health; physically and mentally. I hope to continue being sexually active until my departure from this earthly plane!

Lessons Learned from My Fourth (AND FINAL!) Marriage

I consider my fourth marriage to be a great success story. There are a number of factors that made this relationship different from the others:

1. We didn't have any children living with us. Although Donna and I had daughters from previous marriages, they are now adults living elsewhere. Furthermore, being supportive of them through the years has been a mostly-positive experience as opposed to my earlier problems.

2. Donna is bright and has a wide range of interests similar to my own. Shortly after our marriage, she agreed to retire so we could travel and see the world. A feat that was accomplished with more than sixty cruises over the span of twenty-five years!

3. Donna is a loving and caring person when dealing with other people; including me. She has a great gift of being able to communicate these feelings by word and writing. Her empathy knows no bounds! She is also attractive with a nice figure. This was true the day we first met and is still true to this day. She is exceptionally neat, well groomed, and organized. All features I highly value.

4. We enjoyed an active sex life. Even though this has diminished with time, she was always open to creative ways of keeping the embers glowing. Furthermore, there were no instances of infidelity for either of us. A far cry from my first marriage!

5. Money matters were never a problem. These are openly discussed so both of us know exactly our assets and liabilities. Hence, there are no surprises in this department. With our combined finances we live well and are happy in a beautiful retirement community.

6. One of the key elements of our marriage is the willingness to share our affection for one another. Hugs and kisses are a daily affair as well as holding hands whenever we walk together. These are not perfunctory acts but rather are true signs of our love.

$\mathscr{E}$pilogue

When the first draft of this book was completed, I decided that it would be prudent to include lessons learned for each segment of my life. This turned out to be more difficult than I anticipated. It took considerable effort to distill my thoughts about these events into concise summaries. My hope is that the reader will find these lessons meaningful.

The other point I want to make in this epilogue is that many of the relationship problems that are described in the book were caused by my being naive. I sincerely believe that this was largely corrected in my fourth marriage; hence, the title of this book. As my daughters said -"Dad, you finally got it right!"

Cantos A Mi
Díos

Elba Soler

CANTOS A MI DIOS

Puede hacer pedidos de libros de iUniverse en librerías o poniéndose en contacto con:

iUniverse
1663 Liberty Drive
Bloomington, IN 47403
www.iuniverse.com
1-800-Authors (1-800-288-4677)

ISBN: 978-1-5320-7919-1 (tapa blanda)
ISBN: 978-1-5320-7917-7 (tapa dura)
ISBN: 978-1-5320-7918-4 (libro electrónico)

Número de Control de la Biblioteca del Congreso: 2019910604

Información sobre impresión disponible en la última página.

Fecha de revisión de iUniverse: 07/26/2019

Contents

Introducción

Éste es un libro de poesía que le llegará hasta el corazón y le conmoverá hasta el llanto. Sentirá los más profundos sentimientos encontrados, amor y rencor, ansiedad y liberación…catarsis escrita.

Nací

Nací en la bella isla del encanto: Puerto Rico, USA; a un padre militar. Mis padres se divorciaron cuando yo sólo contaba nueve años. Me sentí desarraigada y tirada de un lado a otro entre ellos y mi abuela. Fuí a nueve escuelas diferentes, lo cual me hizo muy difícil establecer relaciones personales. Durante la etapa del crecimiento me sentí como una flor arrancada, que no pudo florecer; desarraigada y seca, abandonada y olvidada, rechazada y carente de cuidado y afecto…

No teniendo un hogar estable, sentía que no encajaba en ningún sitio, que no pertenecía; me sentía ajena…Hasta que un día leí Juan 14:1-6 y cayó la venda de mis ojos, y abrí los ojos a la verdad. Entonces comprendí: ¡que sí había un lugar para mí, preparado por Jesucristo mismo!

Y no sabiendo cómo expresarme, ni a quién allegarme, vertí mi alma en la poesía. Estos poemas reflejan mi sentir. Lea y sienta…

A Través De Las Lágrimas

A través de las lágrimas
Siente el regocijo,
Recordando
Lo que Jesús dijo:
"No se turbe tu corazón,
Voy a preparar un lugar,
Para que donde yo estoy
Tú también estés conmigo" (Juan 14:1-3)
Te amo tanto,
Que por tí quise
Mi sangre derramar
Para que fueras redimido.
Así que no sea triste tu llanto;
Tu amado se ha ido
A su hogar Celestial,
Para allí esperar
Tu llegada triunfal
Junto conmigo.
Como flores de un día
Que están hoy aquí
Y mañana se han ido,
Así es nuestro duelo
En este suelo.
Halla pues consuelo
En lo que está en el cielo!

Elba Soler
8/20/2013
Valdosta, GA

Adelante – Canto ♫

Adelante,
Quien quiera que sea
Que me esté tocando
Las puertas del alma.
Adelante,
Pues quiero que vea
Que lo estoy queriendo,
Lo estoy esperando,
Con todo mi amor.
No es tan difícil perdonar
Tanta locura,
Que no me importa terminar
En sepultura.
Si ya murió tu viejo amor,
Yo te bendigo.
//Si ya no tienes valor,
Yo sí te doy valor;
Vente conmigo.//

Elba Soler
2/24/2018
Valdosta, GA

Al Cruzar El Puente

Al cruzar el Puente
Que transciende
De una vida sencilla
A otra cometida,
Recuerda el viejo consejo
"Es mejor dar
Que recibir." (Hechos 20:35)
Pronto darás el paso
Que atará el lazo,
Y te has de entregar
De lleno al ser que amas;
Y se han de juntar
Dos cuerpos, dos almas,
Para llenar el vacío
Que todos tenemos.
Así dice la Biblia,
Que Dios dijo:
"No es bueno
Que el hombre esté solo."
Como dos copas a medias,
Para que una pueda rebosar,
Es necesario
Vertir una en la otra;
Darlo todo
Para ser felices.
La vida está llena de matices;
De colores vivos, y también de grises.
Y esos colores se acoplan
Para resaltar el uno al otro.
Tendrán altos y bajos.

Pero si ambos
Comparten un sentimiento,
Y el sólo pensamiento
Es hacer feliz al otro,
Cuando uno caiga en lo bajo,
Tenderá su mano
Para levantarlo,
Y así, su sonrisa viendo,
Los dos al unísono
Terminarán riendo.

Elba Soler
4/2/2004
Valdosta, GA

Al Hijo Pródigo (No Se Puede)

No se puede obtener salvación
Sin pagar el precio:
Redención.
No se puede tener un salvador,
Sin aceptar al Señor:
Jesucristo.
Así Dios lo dispuso
Desde que fundó el mundo.
Si no lo aceptas
Seguirás por la vida
Como un vagabundo;
Andando sin rumbo,
Y dando tumbos,
De izquierda a derecha;
Sin un hogar
Donde descansar.
Habiendo vuelto la espalda
Al que te dió la vida,
Ahora te encuentras
En callejón sin salida.
Nunca encontrarás la puerta
Que da entrada
A la celestial morada
Que para tí está preparada. (Juan 14: 1-6)
Mas si arrepentido
Das vuelta
En tus pisadas,

Dios te acogerá
Con bienvenida
En el paraíso, (Lucas 15:24
Haciendo caso omiso
De todas tus fechorías
Porque te ama en demasía!

Elba Soler
5/29/2005
Valdosta, GA

Angustiosa Ansiedad

Espero pronto poder dejar
El supuesto "lar"
Que logró mantener
Mi torturado ser
En angustioso existir,
En vano vivir.

Es este el "hogar"...
(Quisiera llorar,
Al esta palabra oír,
Y al mismo tiempo reír,
Al yo comprender
Lo que no han de entender:
Y es que es irónico para mí,
Pues no hubo, al fin,
Ni calor, ni hogar,
Ni amor, ni lar,
En este maldito lugar
Que así se hace llamar.)
Mas bien, es el lugar
Donde he llegado a purgar
El pecado de Adán;
Donde habré de dejar
Tantas y tantas perlas
Como para llenar el mar.

Perlas de lágrimas,
Que al rodar por mis mejillas,

Me hicieron pensar
En un día poderme alejar,
Adonde más lejos pudiera llegar,
Y mi felicidad buscar.
Espero este sueño realizar,
Espero poderlo lograr,
Y mi felicidad alcanzar
Antes de marchitar,
Antes de mi vida acabar,
Antes de dejar de soñar…

Elba Soler
9/17/1967. 3:00pm
Río Piedras, PR

Anhelo

Tengo tantos deseos de volver
A mi patria querida!
De ver su brillante sol,
Su cielo azul,
Sus verdes montes.
Sus playas doradas…
Todo, en fin, lo que dejé atrás,
Para venir a esta nación fría.
No me creerás esto,
Pero en estos momentos,
Sin poder contenerme,
Siento rodar por mis mejillas
Las lágrimas saladas.
Rezo diariamente,
Y le pido al Señor,
Que me dé fuerza
Y paciencia para esperar,
Para luchar
Contra mi nostalgia.
El espíritu lucha
Pero la carne es débil.
Cada día flaqueo más y más.
Ya no sé que hacer;
Me consume la nostalgia.
¿Que será de mí?
Sólo puedo rezar y esperar…

Elba Soler - Chicago, IL 1964

Ante Usted

Señor, ante Usted me arrodillo;
No puedo expresar lo que he sentido,
Pero sé que como nave a la deriva
Usted me ha dirigido
Para que no siga perdida.
Ha provisto mi comida,
Y antes de haberlo pedido,
A mi oración ha respondido. (Mateo 21:22)
Porque todas sus ovejas
Llevan su sello
Y Usted cuida de ellas
Con mucho celo. (Juan 10:11)

Elba Soler
Valdosta, GA
3/28/2006

Arenga

¿Porqué criticáis a los otros?
Tal parece que ustedes
Sólo están contentos
En la desgracia de otros.
Y eso yo lo defino
En un sólo término: el odio.

¿Es que acaso la envidia
Ha llegado a tal exremo,
Que si no criticáis a los otros
Con insidia,
Queriendo lastimarles,
No os sentís satisfechos...
Ni tampoco culpables?

Sí; culpables;
Ésa es la verdad escondida;
Aunque no queráis darle pecho;
¡Pobres necios!
En vos está infundida;

Porque os sabéis miserables,
Más despreciables que los otros,
Ante vuestra propia malevolencia,
Propia de nadie.
Sí, vos, con vuestro orgullo,
Sólo sóis eso: nadie.

Jamás podréis ser alguien,
Hasta que humildemente reconozcáis,
Como seres suplicantes,
Y rogando pidáis
La caridad que despreciásteis.
Reconozcan la verdad ante todos,
La verdad innegable,
Dénle pecho al hecho,
Despierten a la realidad palpable;

Reconozcan que sóis seres hambrientos
De amor, de comprensión sedientos,
Ansiosos de cariño;
Y no matéis al niño
Antes de haber nacido;
Sin haber visto la luz,
La Luz redentora de todos,
La Verdad, pseudónima del camino,
Que a la felicidad
Conduce a todos,
Pecadores y místicos;
Pues es común al ser humano,
Si se es reconocido

Ese regalo divino:
La comunión del espíritu
En amor, comprensión y cariño.

Elba Soler
3-20-1967 @5:30pm
Río Piedras, PR

Como Blanca Mariposa

Como blanca mariposa
Que en la flor reposa,
Y de su néctar recibe vigor,
Así reposo yo en mi Señor,
Y de su palabra
Recibo el amor,
Que responde a mi clamor
Y me infunde valor.

Como águila que alza su vuelo,
Se remonta mi alma
Hacia el cielo.
Como la gallina,
Que bajo sus alas
Acoge sus polluelos,
Así el Señor
Cubre mi anhelo
Y me da consuelo.

Como flores de un día,
Que están hoy aquí
Y mañana se han ido,
Así es nuestro duelo
En este suelo.
Halla pues consuelo
En lo que está en el cielo!

Elba R. Soler - 10/31/2006 - Valdosta, GA

Cuando Tú Faltes

Cuando tú faltes
¿Quién ocupará tu lugar?
Porque sólo tú
Eres muy especial.
Yo sólo quiero
El mejor bien para tí
Aunque tú ni siquiera
Te acuerdes de mí.

Tu corazón de piedra
Está entenebrecido
Como lo estaba el mío
Antes de conocer
A Jesucristo.

Me lleno de angustia
Al verte jugando
Con el peligro.
Y al sólo pensar
Que algo pueda
Hacerte algún daño,
Mi alma ya mustia
Por el pesar de los años,
Siente el dolor
Acuchillando.

¿No quieres saber
La promesa de mañana?
No arrojes tu vida
Por la ventana.
Aprovecha tus talentos.
No vivas tan sólo
El placer del momento.
La alegría de hoy
Mañana será lamento.

Elba Soler
5/25/2005
Valdosta, GA

Cuando Yo Me Muera

Cuando yo me muera
No me traigas flores;
Ni tampoco llores.
Porque ya no tendré temores,
Ni sufriré dolores;
Más bien, quiero que ores
Por aquellos que quedan atrás
A merced de las garras
De Satanás;
Que va engañando
Y devorando
A todo aquél que trás él
Su camino va trazando.

Así que regocíjate pensando
Que estoy cantando
Y alabando
Al amor de mis amores;
Acurrucada en el regazo
De mi Padre amado,
Habiéndome colmado
Con el mejor regalo
De su Hijo amado.

Allí, sentado en su trono,
Me dará mi corona,
Mientras mi alma entona,
Como blanca paloma,

Un canto al Dios trino,
Habiéndome limpiado
Y enaltecido
El Dios vivo y divino.

Iré a Él, llena de gozo,   (Apocalipsis 19:7-9)
Vestida como novia en lino fino;
Y Él me recibirá
Mostrando su amor,
Abriendo sus brazos,
Como lo hizo su Hijo
En el crucifijo.

Elba Soler
10/23/2012
Valdosta, GA

©De Colores - Canto ♫

De colores son las flores
Que adornan nuestro lar;
De colores son las flores
Que nos dan dicha sin par;
De colores son las flores
Que florecen sin cesar;
De colores son las flores
Que nos da nuestro padre celestial,
De colores son las flores
Y su nombre quiero ensalzar,
De colores son las flores
Y mi Dios es sin igual.

Elba Soler ©
7/23/2011
Valdosta, GA

Desafío

Así como las olas del mar
Arrastran con la arena,
Así también, siendo aún una nena,
Arrastraron con mi inocencia.

Mas así como el mar bravío
Se estrella contra las rocas,
Así también, enardecida,
Me alzo yo, contra las pasiones locas.

Deseando al fin, sacudirme
De esta vida torcida,
Y así, contrita y arrepentida,
Entrar al cielo, en la otra vida.

Y aunque hoy me quede sola,
No por menos seré vencida;
Mas seré purificada,
Y por mi resistencia, bendecida.

Pues Dios es compasivo,
Y a levantarse ayuda a los caídos,
Contra los que quieren hacer de uno,
Como ellos, seres perdidos.

> *Elba Soler*
> 2/10/1967 San Juan, PR
> Frente a la playa de Dorado

Desde Que Dejé Tu Nido

Dirán que estoy perdido
Desde que dejé tu nido;
Por lo malo que he sido
Mucho he sufrido.
Adonde quiera que he ido,
No me he sentido
Bienvenido.
Nadie me ha acogido;
Como Tú, nadie me ha querido.
No sé lo que me depara el destino,
Ni dónde está escondido,
Aquello que encontrar no he podido.
Pero no me doy por vencido;
Seguiré por muchos caminos
Hasta encontrar mi sino.

Elba Soler
7/7/2013
Valdosta

©Dios Nunca Duerme

Dios nunca duerme,
Nunca descansa;
Nunca se cansa
De oírnos rogar.
Si débil somos,
Él es más fuerte;
Ya no desmayes,
Descansa en Él.

Elba Soler
Valdosta, GA
12/14/2008

Dos Caminos

Eran dos hermanos
Dotados de talento,
Así decía el cuento.
El uno, dedicado a servir a Dios,
Dió gloria por sus logros
Al que todo se lo dió,
Y le seguía bendiciendo.

El otro siguió otro rumbo;
Entregado al mundo,
Cayó en lo más hondo
Y más profundo,
Que es adonde empuja,
(De eso no tenga duda),
Aquél que a nadie ayuda,
Si no es llevarlo a la cima,
Para luego echarlo a la ruina.

Cada cual escoge un camino,
Y al final llega a su destino,
Según lo que haya escogido.

Elba Soler
12/28/2018.
Valdosta, GA

El Espíritu Del Hombre

El espíritu del hombre
Es indomable;
Y esa es nuestra caída.
Queremos dominar
El planeta habitable,
Y sólo somos hormigas.

No nos conformamos
Con lo que tenemos;
Y al cielo queremos
Remontar nuestro vuelo,
Y conquistar el universo,
Por nuestro propio esfuerzo.
En pleno desplego
De orgullo, queremos
Satisfacer nuestro propio ego,
Aún sabiendo
Que es contrario
A Tu divino mandamiento.

En vez de ser sumisos
Hacemos caso omiso
De la voluntad divina.
Así el hombre termina
Segando su propia ruina.
¿Cómo nos atrevemos
A tal desafío?
¿Cómo llegamos
A tal desvarío,
De creer que podemos

Tu gloria alcanzar?
¿De que podemos forjar
Nuestro propio destino,
Siguiendo nuestro camino
Y no aquél
Que nos viniste a mostrar?

Tu palabra nos dice:
"Hay caminos
Que al hombre le parecen bien,
Pero que al final
Llevan a la muerte." (Prov. 14:12)

Pero desechando
Tu sabio consejo
Queremos probar
Nuestra suerte.
Y ahí esta satán,
Para tentarnos.

¿Porqué, mi Dios, eres tardo
En castigarnos?
Me parece oírlo musitar:
"El Señor no es tardo,
Sino que desea
Que todos sean salvos." (2Pe.3:9)

Elba R. Soler
10/31/2006
Valdosta, GA

Él Está Conmigo

Soplan los feroces vientos;
Las tentaciones están ahí;
Pero yo siento paz sabiendo
Que mi Salvador está aquí.
Cuando los "amigos"
Al mundo se han ido,
Y me abandonan al enemigo,
Él me protege del peligro,
Porque Él me ha prometido
Que siempre estará conmigo.

Elba Soler
Valdosta, GA
1/6/2019

El Hombre Sigue Su Empeño

El hombre sigue su empeño
De mejorar el gran diseño
Desplegado en el universo;
El cual es patente
Fué creado por el omnipotente
Y omniciente ingeniero.
¿Pero cómo mejorar
El milagro divino?
El hombre tiene un destino:
Y es el de servir y agradar
Al Dios que todo nos ha dado.
Pero se engaña a sí mismo,
Pensando que los logros,
Que por Su gracia ha alcanzado
Son muestra de su propia estima;
Y queriendo llegar a la cima
Ante el dios Don Dinero
Se ha postrado,
Y así labra el camino
Que lo lleva a su propia ruina.

"Porque espacioso es el camino
Que lleva a la perdición,
Y estrecho el que lleva a la salvación,
Pero pocos lo encuentran."   (Mateo 7:13)

"Esta cosas aborrece Jehová:
Los ojos altivos,
La lengua mentirosa,
Las manos
Que derraman sangre inocente,
El corazón que maquina
Pensamientos inicuos,
Los pies presurosos
Para correr al mal,
Y el que entre sus hermanos
Siembra discordia."   (Proverbios 6:16-19)

Elba Soler
10/31/2006
Valdosta, GA

El Necio

Cada vez que el necio
Desdeña instrucción,
Y desobedece en acción,
Pagará el precio.
Y si rehúsa orar,
El Diablo no es necio,
Y está siempre dispuesto
A su presa acechar.
Porque así está escrito:
"Ancho es el camino
Que lleva a la perdición,
Y estrecho el camino
Que lleva a la salvación;
Pero pocos lo encuentran." (Mateo 7:13)

Elba Soler
Valdosta, GA
3/28/2006

El Poema Más Bello
Creo que nunca he visto
Poema más hermoso y bello
Que un árbol florecido,
Con flores y hojas bien vestido,
Y Con nidos adornando su cabello,
Levantando sus brazos hacia el cielo…

Poemas son creados
Por tontos como yo,
Pero un árbol solo puede crearlo
Un magnífico Dios!

Elba Soler
April 15, 2018.
Valdosta, GA

El Tiempo Pasa Inclemente

El tiempo pasa inclemente;
Por nada, ni nadie se detiene.
Dice la biblia que Cristo viene
Su iglesia a raptar.
Por eso nos debemos preparar.
Porque nadie sabe
Cuando llegará. (Mateo 24:42-51)
Vendrá,
Como ladrón en la noche; (2Pedro 3:10)
Sin ningún reproche.
Y grande será la sorpresa
Para aquellos que Satán
Tiene como presa,
Atados al pecado de Adán.
Pero ya la hora está cerca,
Cuando el Hijo del hombre
Romperá la cadena,
Y nos librará
De nuestra pena
De muerte, y del abismo;
Y con voz más dulce
Que su nombre,
Nos dirá:
"He venido
A tomarlos a mí mismo,
Para que donde yo estoy,
Vosotros estéis conmigo." (Juan 14)
¡Regocijáos en el Paraíso!

Elba Soler 10/31/2006 Valdosta, GA

En la Flor de tu Vida

Estás en la flor de tu vida,
Y tu rosa tendrá espinas;
Cuando te hinque, suspira.
No absandones el sueño
Al cual aspiras.
Como el apóstol Pablo
Soportó el aguijón,   (2 Cor. 12:7-10)
Por amor a Cristo
Coronado de espinas,
Asido al sueño
De entrar a su reino,
Forjado en la victoria vecina.

Elba Soler
Valdosta, GA
10/3/2007

©En la Mañana ♫

En la Mañana al despertar,
Canto a mi Creador.
Rodeada de mi soledad,
Clamo al Consolador.
Al enfrentar la adversidad,
Confiaré en mi Salvador.

Y Él que es fiel y verdadero
Allí estará y me consolará.
//En el día venidero
Él no me fallará…\\

Hay quien adora el dinero,
Mas yo amo a Dios primero.
Hay quien busca la fama,
Mas yo sigo al que me ama.
Hay quien no teme a nada,
Mas yo temo al que me guarda.

Y Él que es fiel y verdadero
Allí estará y me consolará.
//En el día venidero
Él no me fallará…\\

Elba R. Soler
Valdosta, GA
6/24/2012

63

En Vano

En vano
Y muy ufano
Se afana el hombre en su labor.
En su ignorancia desdeña
Tu infinito amor.
Se arrastra como gusano
Y desprecia
De tu mano
Tu divino regalo
De redención.
Con jactancia
Se empeña
En comprar la salvación,
Que tú mismo
Haciéndote humano
Pagaste en la crucifixión.

Elba Soler
10/31/2006
Valdosta, GA

FE

Dios: ¿Dónde estás;
Dónde te escondes...?
¿Porqué a mi llamado
No respondes?

Dios: te siento
Ante mí latente;
Cerca, omnipresente...
Mas trato de alcanzarte,
Y de pronto desapareces...

June 1968
Chicago, IL

Eres intangible,
Espíritu invisible,
Mas sé que eres
Y existes;

Por eso mi llamado persiste;
Porque tú mismo dijiste:
"Persevera y ten fe,
¡Y yo te habré de responder!"

Elba Soler
Jueves 9/26/1968
Chicago, IL

67

Gracias Señor

Gracias Señor,
Que todo provees.
Gracias por la comida
Que me dá alimento,
Me sirve de sustento
Y me dá la vida.
Gracias por el techo
Que me cobija.
Gracias por la ropa
Que mi desnudez
Mantiene vestida;
Y el calzado
Que protege mis pies.
Gracias, porque nada
Me ha faltado,
Ni una sola vez;
Hambre no he pasado,
Ni siquiera sed.
Gracias, Señor,
Por todo lo bueno y bello
Que nos has dado.
Pero aun así,
De tu lado
Nos hemos apartado;
Despreciamos tu divino regalo
Y buscamos lo malo.
Mas para tí,
Seguimos siendo
Lo más amado…

¿Cómo explicarlo?
Tanto amor
Sin pedir nada a cambio.
Sólo un Dios
Infinitamente amoroso
Y misericordioso
Como Tú
Puede hacerlo.
Alabado seas,
Mi Señor Jesús.

Elba Soler
5/23/2010
Valdosta, GA

Gracias, Padre Santo

Gracias, Padre Santo,
Por estos alimentos;
Porque siempre
Provees mi sustento;
Y confío que así sea
En todo momento,
Hasta mi último aliento.

Donde quiera que miro
Se manifiesta tu grandeza;
Por eso yo admiro
Tu hermosura y tu belleza.

Al contemplar tu creación
Me lleno de emoción
Y me pongo a pensar:
¡Qué gran imaginación!

¡Qué gran ingeniero
Y arquitecto,
Para diseñar con sabiduría
Y precisión,
Todo en armonía
Y perfección!

Elba Soler
11/25/2015
Valdosta, GA

©Hoy Es Mi Cumpleaños 🎵

Hoy es mi cumpleaños,
Y yo le quiero cantar
A Dios todopoderoso
Que me vino a salvar.

Hoy es mi cumpleaños,
Y gracias le quiero dar
Por el mejor regalo
Que es la vida eternal.

Hoy es mi cumpleaños,
A mi Dios yo quiero alabar,
Porque el amor que Él me ha dado
Nadie me lo puede dar.

Hoy es mi cumpleaños,
De mi vida terrenal,
Y como son muchos años,
Ya no los voy a contar!

Elba Soler
Valdosta, GA
7/1/2012

La Felicidad

La felicidad es algo
Que creamos en la mente.
No es algo que se busca,
Y es difícil que se encuentre.
Es despertar
Y el día comenzar
Contando nuestras bendiciones;
De rodillas orando,
Desechando el deseo
De tener lo que no tenemos,
Y haciendo lo mejor
Con lo que sí tenemos.
Es saber que la vida
Ha sido diseñada para nosotros,
Por el gran creador;
Persistiendo en la tarea
Sin ninguna queja.
Porque es completando
Lo que Dios nos ha asignado
Que realmente encontramos
La felicidad que buscamos.

Elba Soler
10/3/2007
Valdosta, GA

Las Manos Del Tiempo

Las manos del tiempo
Se mueven incesantes,
Inclementes y arrogantes,
Dejando atrás una interrogante.

Si tuviésemos sensatez,
Y un granito de fe,
Aprovecharíamos todo momento
Siguiendo el ejemplo
Del gran maestro:
"Aprovechando el tiempo
Porque los días son malos"   (Efesios 5:16)
He aquí, el tiempo ha pasado;
¿Cómo seremos hallados?

¿Estaremos preparados,
Como la novia esperando
Al esposo amado?
Ese fué su regalo:
Un legado
De esperanza,
Amor y sabiduría.

Elba Soler
10/31/2006
Valdosta, GA

79

Más que Nada

Crucificado,
Rechazado y desolado,
Vivió para morir
Por los damnificados.
Como una rosa
En el suelo pisoteada,
Tomo la caída,
Más que nada,
Pensando en mí.

Elba Soler
2/18/2017
Valdosta, GA

Mi Fiel Amigo

Yo trabajo
Para un carpintero,
Pero no por dinero,
Si no porque lo quiero;
Porque Él me amó
A mí primero.

Él siempre me ha cuidado,
Aún cuando yo
Le he faltado;
Él siempre está a mi lado,
Aunque yo
Lo haya olvidado.

Él siempre ha sido
Mi fiel amigo;
Ha sido bueno conmigo,
Aunque no lo he merecido,
Y no le haya seguido.

Pero yo en Él confío
A plenitud,
Porque aún pasada
Mi juventud.
Él no me echa al olvido.

Yo sé que lo he herido.
Lo he hecho llorar;
Y he visto
Sus lágrimas derramar,
Copiosamente cayendo
Desde arriba;
Pero aún yendo
Como nave a la deriva,
Él me está viendo,
Y me cuida, y me abriga.
Si no fuera por Él,
Mi JesuCristo,
¿Qué haría?

Elba Soler
Valdosta, GA
1/5/2013

Mucho Me Has Dado

De lo mucho que me has dado,
Poco te devuelvo;
Por eso te amo,
porque aunque yo no reclamo,
Tú me sigues bendiciendo.

Aunque yo entregara
Todo lo que tengo,
No sería ni un céntimo
De todo lo que me regalas.
Por eso tu nombre yo bendigo,
Porque tú me has bendecido;
No porque lo haya merecido
Sino por tu amor infinito y bendito.
Gracias, Dios mío,
Por tu Hijo, JesuCristo!

Elba R. Soler
11/25/2015
Valdosta, GA

O Acaso en el Ocaso

Al rayar el alba
Y despuntar la aurora,
El rocío llora de alegría.
Las aves cantan
Con algarabía,
Rompiendo el silencio
De la noche oscura;

Anunciando la llegada
De un Nuevo día,
En la hora matutina
Nace la esperanza,
En la mañana pura,
Cuando la vista alcanza
Al astro sol
Vestido de oro,
Opacando el negro tesoro,
Bordado manto
De diamantes,
Que brillan con la luna,
Que arropaba con ternura
Los sueños de mi cuna.

Al marchar el día,
Enfrento nuevas aventuras,
Y también desventuras.
Mas no por eso devaneo;

Si no sigo segura,
Que allá en la altura
Hay alguien que me cuida.
Por eso canto a mi Señor
Con gratitud muda.
¿O acaso en el ocaso
No cantan también los pájaros
Alabando al Creador?

Entonces también yo,
En lo alto y lo profundo,   (Romanos 8:38)
En lo claro y lo oscuro,
Daré gracias al Señor;
Alabando su grandeza,
Cantando sus proezas,
Y reciprocando su amor.

Elba Soler
10/31/2006
Valdosta, GA

Padre Nuestro

Fuerte nos azotas,
Al parecer a tu antojo,
Mas sé que es santo tu enojo
Y al que amas disciplinas;
Castigas como medicina,
Corriges nuestros errores,
Nuestros pasos encaminas
Y calmas nuestros temores.

Por eso nos dijo
Tu amado Hijo,
Maestro divino,
Al orar así hacedlo:
"Padre nuestro,
Que estás en los cielos…"
Porque grande es
Tu amor paternal,
Fiel, infinito y eternal;
Con nada terrenal
Se puede comparar.

Elba Soler
10/31/2006
Valdosta, GA

Palabra vana

Palabra vana es la del hombre.
Si te deja, no te asombre.
Siempre en busca de placeres
Y nuevos horizontes,
Y aventuras en la vida,
Pronto se olvida
De las promesas,
A las que no responde.

Aún cuando comiendo a tu mesa,
Sacia su hambre perversa,
Y luego, ni te mira.
No limites tu horizonte
Hasta donde
La vista alcanza.
Sube al monte
Y descansa,
Lejos del mundo;
Busca la bienaventuranza.

Elba R. Soler
10/3/2007
Valdosta, GA

Por Mí Ciega Rebeldía

Señor,
Antes de conocerte
Pensaba que mi vida
Era como una pequeña isla
De complacencia,
Rodeada por un océano
De tristeza.
Pero ahora que te he conocido,
He comprendido,
Y digo, que mi vida
Fue una isla de pobreza,
Rodeada por un mar de riquezas.
Porque Satanás
Me tenía oprimida
Y sometida
A la pobreza espiritual,
Por mi ciega rebeldía;
Mientras tú me ofrecías
Riqueza celestial.
Sólo tenía
Que hacer una decisión,
Para recibir el milagro
De la transformación.
Ahora en vez de mendigar,
Contigo voy a reinar
En el paraíso eternal.

Elba Soler 1/16/2009 Valdosta, GA

Quebranto

Mi alma está llena de pesar,
Que sólo Dios puede aliviar.
Yo le quisiera cantar,
Pero siento mi voz quebrar
Por el peso de mi quebranto,
Que quiere romper en llanto.

Por el mundo errante
He ido rodando,
Siempre buscando
Un ser amante.
Pero ni perlas, ni diamantes,
Lo hace a uno digno
Del gran estandarte.

Sólo Dios puede cambiar
El barro en vasija fina,
Y llenarla con agua viva
Que rebosa de vida,
Como la llovizna matutina
Que dá a la hierba yerta
Color y vida,
Como el rocío
Llena el vacío
De las hojas muertas…

Elba Soler
4/10/2011
Valdosta, GA

©Quién Nos Apartará-Canto ♫

Quién nos apartará
Del amor de Cristo?
Quién nos impedirá
Recibir su perdón?
Quién nos separará
Del amor divino,
Del que por mí vino
A la crucifixión?

Si //Dios sabe que lo quiero//
//Con todo el corazón//
//Si Él es la esperanza//
//Y mi única ilusión//
//Es que Él me bendiga//
Tan sólo con su amor,
//Es todo lo que ansía//
Mi pobre corazón.

Jamás habrá quien me ame
Como Cristo me ha querido,
Porque ese amor divino,
Ni aún fingido
Tiene comparación.

Si…

Elba Soler
Sun 4/15/2018
Valdosta, GA

Sí Al Señor Entregas

Si al Señor
Entregas tus peces,
Él los multiplicará con creces.
Si tu vida ofreces,
Siendo fiel a Su llamado,
Y sigues al Salvador,
Predicando en su nombre,
Él te hará pescador
De hombres.

No te niegues
A la brega;
Tu vida entrega,
Como Él entregó la suya,
Y verás como siegas
Gran buenaventura.
Deja atrás la bulla
Que el mundo te ofrece,
Con artificios y engaños,
Y que al fin,
Termina en llanto.

Elba R. Soler
Valdosta, GA
5/6/2009

Vente Conmigo

Dios lo vió cansado,
La cura no había conseguido.
Entonces lo abrazó, y dijo,
"Vente conmigo."

Con corazones llorosos, lo vimos,
Poco a poco desfallecer;
Aunque lo amábamos muchísimo,
Lo encomendamos al Altísimo.

Descansaron las manos
Que trabajaron con tesón;
Cesó de latir su gran corazón…
Dios rompió nuestro corazón
Para probar que Él
Se lleva lo mejor!

Elba Soler
Valdosta, GA
9/11/2015

Verde Esperanza

Que tu cielo sea
Verde esperanza
Y tu horizonte
Hasta donde
Tu vista alcanza.
Que todo lo que veas
Sea belleza
Y hermosura;
Y toda agua que bebas
Sea dulce y pura.
Recuerda siempre
Que aunque la vida quebranta
Si acudes a Cristo
Él te levanta!

Elba Soler
10/31/2006
Valdosta, GA

Ya No Estoy Sola

Aunque te hayas ido,
Recordaré lo que me habías dicho:
"Ya no está sola."
Sólo que ahora he comprendido,
Que aunque ya no cuento contigo,
Puedo depender de mi fiel amigo:
Jesucristo;
Quien por mí dió su vida,
Y por su sangre vertida
Fuí redimida,
Y aún después de su partida
Ha quedado su Espíritu,
Para darme consuelo
Cuando recuerdo:
¡Que ya no estoy sola!

Elba R. Soler
Valdosta, GA
10/31/2006

©Ya No Estoy Sola-Canto ♫

Ya no estoy sola,
Ya nunca más volveré a estar sola;
Ahora sé que tu siempre
Llenarás mi soledad.

Tú has venido
Para siempre a mi vida,
Has sanado mi herida
Y ya jamás ha de sangrar.

A tu amor mi cariño
Se aferró desesperadamente,
Y ya sé porque tus labios
Pronunciaron el adiós…

Ahora, mi vida,
Ya no estoy sola,
Ya nunca más volveré a estar sola,
Porque tengo en la vida
A mi Santo Consolador.

Elba R. Soler
Valdosta, GA
10/31/2006

111

Ya No Lloro (Mi Tesoro)

Ya no lloro,
Porque tengo el tesoro
Que más valoro:
Saber que cuando oro,
Me escucha
El que me dió la vida,
Y no me olvida,
Si no, que me convida
A compartir con Él
Su riqueza Divina.

Elba Soler
Valdosta, GA
8/15/ 2017

Salmo 40:1-8 (Parafraseado)

Apresúrate Señor, a ayudarme.
Confunde a los que me quieren destruir.
Porque me rodean muchos males ;
La iniquidad se ha apoderado de mí.
Mi corazón te ha faltado;
No me atrevo a levantar mi vista.
Mas tu verdad yo he declarado,
Tu fidelidad y salvación
Delante de la congregación,
Y a seguirte estoy lista.
No me niegues tu amor,
Pues grande es tu misericordia.
Ténme paciencia y compasión;
Tú me sacaste de la horrible fosa,
Y limpiaste el barro de mis pies.
Me pusiste sobre la Roca,
Y encaminaste mi senda.
Pusiste nuevo canto en mi boca;
Bendita soy porque confío en Usted.
No quisiste sacrificio ni ofrenda.
Mis oídos abriste
Y se me cayó la venda.
Vine a tí, y entonces ví,
Que allí en tu libro
Mi nombre estaba ahí.

Elba Soler
1/11/2009
Valdosta, GA

115

Printed in the United States
By Bookmasters